# Compelling

## The Fight for a Faith School

**Dr Cheron Byfield & Ralph Turner**

malcolm down
PUBLISHING

# Commendations

The guiding hand of God shines through this book. *Compelling* charts the challenging birth pains of this Christian business school in the heart of the second largest city in the UK. Cheron's story is that of courageous advocacy for social justice, be it in her ministry in the Black Boys Can projects, Excell3 or in King Solomon International Business School. The school's continued and mounting challenges came fast and furious: heads upon heads, portacabins and building works, letters of betrayal, false allegations and heavy scrutiny by Ofsted. Having the support of the Prime Minister and his ministers of state could not prevent the level of opposition Cheron and the project faced from civil servants. I highly recommend reading this account of unquenchable faith, hope and courage if you are looking for inspiration, a radically new way of bringing God into the heart of a Christian school, as well as preparing students to succeed in an increasingly competitive and global marketplace. If you want to be inspired, touch the flame of hope or receive courage, then I highly recommend reading *Compelling*.
**Chris Wright, Director of Education, Woodard Schools**

This compelling book provides insight into the journey and operations of this unique and much-needed school. It captures the long and enormously challenging journey of establishing mainstream academy schools that so many members of the Windrush generation and their descendants have experienced. Its accuracy exposes the stereotypical views of those in positions of political power and gives weight to the conspiracy theorists that there is an agenda to keep marginalised communities in their place, and that place excludes them from being mainstream providers. Is important that we give due credit to Dr Cheron Byfield and the team for their resilience and for the great legacy of King Solomon International Business School. As God is on the side of justice, we must continue to fight for justice. **Bishop Dr Desmond Jaddoo, Chair, Windrush National Organisation**

*Compelling* is the manual for anyone with a God-sized dream and a passion for changing lives. Through the raw emotions of frustration, disappointment and tear-jerking moments of triumph, Cheron demonstrates what it means to live by faith and model Christ, even through adversity and fierce opposition. Through her inspiring leadership, Cheron and her team have transformed the lives of children and communities for the better, forever, while proving the merits of combining academics, business acumen, strong moral character and, most importantly, unconditional love in the approach to education. A fantastic read of courage from start to finish. **Dr Andrea Taylor-Cummings, TEDx speaker, Author and Co-Founder, The4Habits.com**

This riveting book offers an absorbing insight into the struggle for acceptance by the authorities of an innovative new Christian school. The international business and enterprise specialism at the heart of the vision of this school is an inspiringly positive approach. Although initially decried as a bit 'revolutionary' by traditional educationalists, post-Brexit/post-Covid career opportunities demand new approaches from schools. This school is ahead of the game. It is stretching our youngsters to embrace international business and entrepreneurship, underpinned by Christian business principles, and to develop the skills that will enable them to work, trade and thrive in a worldwide free-market economy. The creativity that is being nurtured is evident, even in the primary school, and will pay dividends to our society. **Peter Le Brocq, Secretary of the Christian Business Men's Fellowship International and Professional Mechanical Engineer (Retired)**

Cheron's God-endowed vision and giftedness is clearly identified, nurtured, honed, and then set on a trajectory and orbit that would encounter and break through barriers. How then does she collaborate, to navigate systemic principalities, hegemonic structures, and negative predispositions, to actualise the 'promised land of educational excellence' for children, in particular black and marginalised young people? Will she maintain her God-given vision, values and virtues? Will the seeds of God-given principles, overarching wit and wisdom be sowed in the soil of the intellects and souls? *Compelling: The Fight for a Faith School* is a 'must read' for academics and non-academics, people of faith and none, alike. It is transcultural in its background, geopolitical in its scope, spiritually and ethically balanced and focused. I wholeheartedly commend this book. **Bishop Tedroy M. Powell, President of Pentecostal and Charismatic Forum for Churches Together in England and Chair of West Midlands Faith in Action**

The development of King Solomon International Business School should be read and understood from a number of perspectives. It is a story of resilience, forbearance, growth, triumph and disappointment. It should be used as a reference by other marginalised communities wishing to become mainstream providers. Although the progenitors of this school come from a committed Christian background, that should not be used to cloud the essential lessons of this book. At its core are issues of race, gender, religious discrimination and low expectations. It is a clear example of the intersectional relationship between different aspects of societal oppression. But perhaps the most troubling part is the illusion of entry and acceptance at the point of increased curtailment and control. **Chester Morris, Former Local Authority Principal Education Officer and Additional Ofsted Inspector**

# Commendations

As a member of Generation Z, I can categorically say this story needed to be told. It's phenomenal. Amidst all of the challenges the school faced, it has transformed and impacted on so many lives. The testimonies and poems from students, staff and others are amazing. Without this book my generation would never know or understand the depth of the struggles Dr Byfield, the team and other black pioneers who have dared to enter the unwelcoming and hostile mainstream education sector as providers, had to endure. It's shocking to discover the racism, sexisim and religious discrimination that still exists behind the scenes in the education establishment. Thanks for sharing your story. My generation of young people need to know your experiences. It's empowering. It's our legacy. **Nicole Taylor BEM, one of the youngest recipients listed in the 2022 Queen's Honours list**

This book is a living testimony of all that exceptional educational and entrepreneurial women leaders such as Dr Cheron Byfield have had to endure, fight against and overcome. There has been endless barriers, setbacks and unfair decisions to deal with in order to take up a rightful place as a mainstream educational provider. A lesser woman, a lesser team of supporters, a lesser people without faith in a power greater than themselves, would have given up a long time ago. But that is not our story. The ongoing struggle for better learning and enterprise outcomes for inner-city children from disadvantaged communities, especially black children, in line with a Christian faith, is truly a compelling story that should challenge the educational institution to change its race equality policy and practice as well as touch and uplift those on the side of equality and justice. **Patricia Lamour MBE, CEO, Aspire Education Group Ltd**

Faith has long played a role in the inception and development of educational policies and practices within the UK. The fact that its place has increasingly been lost does not mean it is no longer relevant. The story of King Solomon International Business School is a testament to the vision, wisdom, courage and indefatigability of the passion of a woman and her team to see the Christian faith embedded and outworked in the culture of a contemporary school environment. The twists and turns of a story that reminds the reader of David's battle with Goliath, is filled with suspense. The challenges remind us that there is much work to do when it comes to faith in education.

**Revd David Shosanya, Principal of Paideia Training & Consultancy and Founder of The Ministers' Appreciation Ball**

I remember well my visit to King Solomon International Business School for their 2019 Matriculation Service. The school was amazing and the pupils were happy. I also noticed a strong, unapologetic Christian ethos in the school which is also reflected in this book. It is quite unusual and remarkable that a school's values and ethos should be informed by the Fruit of the Spirit. Dr Cheron Byfield is a Christian educationalist with a strong faith and determination to build something of worth and value that would benefit the whole community. Her faith in God and her professionalism has enabled the school to provide a training ground for the next generation of ethical and socially responsible business women and men. This book tells the story of this school's journey with honesty and integrity. I highly commend the book, and pay tribute to Cheron's extraordinary work, vision and leadership, and for delivering an educational legacy.

**Dr R. David Muir, Head of Whitelands College, University of Roehampton**

Commendations

The establishment of King Solomon International Business School was not just a miracle but a spiritual revolution. The very heart of the gospel of our Christ (Matthew 19:14) expresses the heart of our Lord Jesus Christ that little children are at the very centre of the kingdom of God. The establishment of King Solomon was fulfilling this great commission. A place of light in a world that is getting darker and darker for children. As a doctor and a physician psychiatrist I and my colleagues have had to treat many children and teenagers confused and traumatised by the ever-intrusive social media. King Solomon is a refuge, where academic excellence is pursued and children are nurtured to develop exemplary character based on the virtues associated with the Fruit of the Spirit.
**Dr Christopher Oyede MBBS, MD, Chief of Psychiatry**

This is indeed a very captivating, inspirational, and thought-provoking book. We thank God for giving the authors the wisdom and guidance to tell this powerful story, which demonstrates that Christianity is a living faith that brings hope, salvation and restoration, even in the education marketplace. Despite its many challenges, King Solomon has been blessed by the Christian ethos that continues to shape, encourage and empower young minds to develop and be better citizens now and in the future. These students will go on to have a positive impact on others in their communities. There is undoubtedly a need for more schools like King Solomon International Business School throughout this country. Its journey so far is indeed compelling. God's purposes are unstoppable. We wait in great anticipation to see this school's future unfold.
**Dr Beverly Lindsay OBE, OD, Founder and General Manager of Diamond Travels**

Purpose, passion and serving others, when combined, leads to something quite compelling. Something the world needs. To compel

leaves an impression, and is so powerful that the agent will stop at nothing to see vision become reality. This must-read book is not merely a story of a faith school opening, but an example of the determination to not let go of God through any valley, shadow or criticism. Dr Cheron, besides evoking the interest of every other pioneer, shows how to lead by the courage of your convictions. Be compelled!
**Revd Jonny Lee, Senior Pastor, Renewal**

Cheron reminds me of a couple who moved from the UK to West Africa, and started an all-through school, producing students for Harvard, Oxford and Cambridge. They said that had they remained in the UK they would not have been able to achieve this. I pray for the day when politicians and their officers in this nation will begin to have the foresight to recognise the talents and gifts of all its citizens and to use them to develop and make significant improvements in communities and the nation. I want to remind Cheron and every person who has passion, zeal and commitment to a worthy goal to never give up but to continue to empower their communities. God has given you the tenacity to withstand, to rise above, to continue to forge ahead and to establish your purpose for your generation and generations to come.
**Revd Les Isaacs OBE, Founder of Ascension Trust and Pioneer of Street Pastors**

Despite the challenges faced by Cheron Byfield and her colleagues, it is encouraging to read about their tenacity and faith, driven by a sense of purpose, to set up a Christian Faith School in the West Midlands. The Christian characteristics of the school were certainly not a threat to social cohesion, but an asset. The many stories of the work with the children, parents and staff of all faith and non, demonstrates the power of Jesus' love. Their engagement in the wider community shows the important role that schools can play in society. The government should be supporting schools like King Solomon that are making such a significant impact on the lives of children, their families and society. Those involved in establishing and working in the school are to be applauded for making such an impact. I hope the future sees this good work being successfully built on.

**Revd Paul Rochester, General Secretary of Free Churches Group**

First published 2022 by Malcolm Down Publishing Ltd.

www.malcolmdown.co.uk

25 24 23 22     7 6 5 4 3 2 1

British Library Cataloguing in Publication Data
A catalogue record for this book is available from the British Library.

ISBN 978-1-912863-83-9

Illustrated by Lizzy Standbrook www.lizzystandbrook.com

Cover design by Esther Kotecha

Art direction by Sarah Grace

Printed in the UK

# Dedication

This book is dedicated to some very special students:

**The Founding students of 2015.** They will always be remembered for being pioneers. Their names are listed towards the back of this book.

**Year 11 Alumni who graduated from the school in 2020 and 2021.** They are an exceptional group of students. They are not only trail blazers, but they have learnt to be highly resilient amidst various challenges, to bounce back in the event of adversity, to cope with and rise to inevitable challenges, problems and setbacks and to come back stronger from them.

And finally, this book is dedicated to all the **current and future students** of King Solomon International Business School. May the Lord bless you and keep you and cause His face to shine upon you and give you peace.

# Thank You

**Thank you from Cheron**

Thanks to Ralph for capturing the story of King Solomon International Business School in a way that brings glory to God.

Thanks to all those who have played a long, sustained and significant role in the school's journey, namely Audrey Taylor – my sister and prayer partner; my family; the founding directors – Carol Brown, Clive Bailey, Dr Mark Yeadon who joined shortly afterwards; and Revd David Illingworth – a Trust member. Thanks also to Excell3 board members and staff at King Solomon who have served for seven years. Sincere gratitude also to Chris Wright and the Woodard Corporation, Bishop Wilton Powell OBE, and the Order of St Leonard.

The school could not have survived so much turbulence without strong prayer support, so thanks to Pastor Doreen Makaya and the school's chaplaincy team, the parent prayer group and staff prayer group. Thanks to the Trust members – Dr Sola Adesola, Dr Beverly Lindsay OBE, OD, DL, as well as to the prayer support of friends of the school – Joyce Fletcher and her prayer team, Gwendolyn Daley JP, MBE and her prayer teams, the prayer teams at House of Praise, Acocks Green and Farm Street churches, Pray for School, John and Margaret Walton, Jacee Carter, Inderjit Bhogal, and the West Midlands Faith in Action.

There are so many friends of the school, but some have been directly involved in supporting us through difficult times, including Dr Cllr Yvonne Mosquito, Jill Saunders, Lin Rowe, Brigitta Goff and the school's neighbour, Lodge Tyres.

Thanks to Baroness Berridge, David Cameron and all the officers within the Department for Education that have been supportive of King Solomon.

Thanks to all our former and current members, directors, senior leaders, staff, consultants, associates, volunteers and interns that have contributed to the development of this school.

Thanks to the late Gerry Goddard and John Gibson for the invaluable roles they played in the early life of the school. They are gone, but not forgotten. Rest in peace.

And finally, a huge thanks to all the founding parents of 2015; you are truly pioneers. God bless you and your children and their children.

## Thank you from Ralph

My thanks to Cheron and her amazing team at King Solomon School for allowing me to help tell their story. Grateful thanks to all the staff and directors at King Solomon who spoke with me or sent through recorded interviews. Thank you to Lizzy Standbrook for the book cover illustration. Thank you to Nathan Turner for his time and educational expertise in proofreading the book. Thanks to Malcolm and the team at MDP. Thank you to the friends and family that are part of the amazing Chroma Church Leicester. And thanks, as always, to my wife Rohini for her love and support.

# Contents

**The Fight For Justice**

**Reflections On The Fight**

# Foreword

As General Secretary of Churches Together in England it gives me great pleasure to write the foreword for *Compelling*, an insightful, powerful and highly inspirational book about King Solomon International Business School. This book is a celebration of an extraordinary school that stands as a beacon on the horizon. It charts the immense challenges and triumphs of the school and is written with integrity and honesty by Dr Cheron Byfield and Ralph Turner.

It's been a joy over nearly twenty years of ministry in Birmingham, to see the development of organisations pioneered by Cheron, including Excell3, Black Boys Can and King Solomon International Business School. I first met the inspirational Dr Cheron Byfield nearly two decades ago, when I was National Director of Transforming Lives for Good, an education charity partnering with churches to run alternative education schools and early intervention programmes for pupils at risk of exclusion from school throughout the UK. Cheron has a deep passion for the education of children and young people, and so does Ralph Turner, the co-author of Compelling. Ralph spent years serving as a school governor and chair of a governing body in a secondary school. He is also a prolific author of a number of Christian autobiographies, including Greater Things – the story of the New Wine Movement, another organisation I have first-hand knowledge of. Ralph's God given writing skills has been capitalised on to bring extraordinary stories of ordinary Christian people to life and those skills shine through the presentation of this book.

I have always been struck by the Victor Hugo quote 'He who opens a school, closes a prison'. So it was my great pleasure to have been invited to the official opening of King Solomon International Business School several years ago, a school committed to closing the doors of prison.

What I saw when I visited the school that day, is very much captured in this book - that is an all-through, multi-denominational Christian school that was pursing educational excellence, developing students with exemplary character and equipping them to be able to live, work and trade in the global economy, and to be successful.

This unapologetic Christian school not only strives to provide a great education but equally important, it focuses on development of the character of its students. The brutal war which commenced in 2022 between Russia and the Ukraine serves to remind us just how important character development is. There is no better framework to develop character than that associated with the values of the Fruit of the Spirit, the values used in the school. The world undoubtedly needs more Christian schools like King Solomon.

Through the pages of this book, the practical and powerful outworking of the Christian faith and the compassion shown to its students is clearly evident, irrespective of their faith or ideology. I personally, during my visit, witnessed a school genuinely committed to educating marginalised groups including black pupils. This is not something you necessarily encounter often in the British education system. It's no wonder I saw such buy-in from a host of stakeholders, including the local politicians, church and community leaders, educationalists and most importantly, parents. This was no ordinary school. Indeed it was Rosalie Jones, not a celebrity, but an elderly widow, who had made a donation to the school from the little she had, that was chosen to pronounce the official opening of the school. This spoke volumes about the schools Christian values.

The book tells the story of a Christian school rooted in the community. Throughout the book you will hear the voices of the whole community – the children, staff, parents, trustees, members, Christian community, black community, business community, international community. Their poems, prayers, and powerful testimonies are insightful and inspiring. You will also learn about the high aspiration it has for its students, which I can testify to, having seen the images of successful Christian billionaires in one of its corridors of fame. It gives a clear message to students that they can achieve the extraordinary.

The authors provide insight into the controversy, opposition, rejection, politics, injustice, betrayal, and turbulence that Dr Byfield and the team experienced. Each section of the book conveys the continual and vicious battles they had to fight.

Churches Together in Britain and Ireland (CTBI) along with Churches Together in England (CTE), highlight Racial Justice Sunday each year. This book will be a constant reminder of the need for racial justice to be front and centre of those who are followers of Christ as well as our colleagues that are committed to human rights, because to ignore it is simply to miss the elephant in the room!

Undoubtedly this story needed to be told. It's an important part of our history. In oral tradition, important moments of history can so easily be lost, but God opened the door for this book to be written. Big lessons can be learnt from this small book. Within it are lessons and reference points for policy makers, civil servants, schools and Christian schools, the government, Christians, non-Christians, other faiths, visionaries and the current and future generations of Black and ethnically diverse communities. Academics and leaders too will find the book to be a useful study.

Christians will be inspired and challenged to be salt and light in the marketplace. Those who have lost sight of their dreams will be energised to dream again. Whether you are thinking of starting your own business, considering a profession in education or starting an initiative to enable your local community to thrive, this highly inspiring book will propel you to keep on going when things get tough, and even when all appears to be lost.

In closing, *Compelling* is a compelling story that absolutely lives up to its title. Once you pick up the book it's difficult to put down. In places it reads like a suspense thriller and ends with a great cliff hanger - what will happen to this incredible school next?

As Christians we stand united with King Solomon International Business School as it pursues its compelling Christian vision.

I've finished the preamble so it's time for you to climb on board. You're in for a roller coaster ride! Be inspired. Be challenged. Be blessed. Be compelled.

**Bishop Mike Royal, General Secretary, Churches Together in England**

# Introduction

'It's not fair, it's just not fair!'

Dr Cheron Byfield was having a bad day. Frustration and disappointment seemed to be stalking her. At every turn, her vision for a Christian-based school in Birmingham had been thwarted.

And now her trusted political associate, let's call her Bethany, was insisting she went to yet another meeting with yet more government officials.

Cheron was on her way home from work when she received the call from Bethany. Cheron had received an invitation to a meeting with Baroness Warsi. Bethany was shocked with Cheron's seemingly dismissive attitude towards the invite.

'Cheron, an invite directly from Baroness Warsi! She's a senior government minister, the Minister for Faith, and you're not going?'

'Bethany, I'm honoured to be invited, really I am, but I've got so much work to do. I'll make sure a member of my staff attends though.'

'No, Cheron, you've got to go!' Bethany was very persuasive. And in the end, it was enough. Cheron agreed.

The venue for the meeting was embargoed until the next day.

The following morning the address was released. It was in Birmingham and in an office complex at the bottom of the road from where Cheron worked. Cheron couldn't believe it. Two minutes and she'd be there!

Later that afternoon Cheron found herself pulling into the office complex. She knew it well of course. And that's why she noticed how different everything looked that day. The office was generally teeming with people. The car park was usually full.

But there were hardly any cars around. No one to see either. Except two police cars driving past. Two at once. That was a bit strange.

Cheron knocked on the door rather tentatively. It opened an inch or two.

'Yes, who are you? What are you here for?'

Not the kindest of greetings. And strange to see such caution on display for what was simply another government meeting in this interminable trail of meetings that had littered Cheron's life for several years now.

'Er, I'm here to see Baroness Warsi. For a meeting.'

'Ah yes, that's fine. Do come in.'

As Cheron walked into the building, there were a few people chatting and drinking coffee. Cheron recognised the Baroness and walked towards her.

'Hello, who have you come to see?'

Cheron was a little flummoxed by this question.

'Well . . . you actually.'

'No, you haven't. No.' Baroness Warsi smiled. 'You've come to see David Cameron, the Prime Minister.'

The day got stranger still. Cheron and the other invited guests were ushered into a boardroom and Cheron found herself sitting next to the Baroness in the meeting, with the Prime Minister directly opposite her.

The Baroness had briefed the guests on how to address the Prime Minister. Each guest would be given the opportunity to raise one issue about their organisation. Cheron's turn came.

'Prime Minister, my ongoing frustration is in trying to start a Christian faith school. We have been pushed back so many times now. We are doing all the right things, passing all the needed consent processes, but still, we are not getting through to final approval.'

'That just shouldn't be the case,' said the Prime Minister. Turning to Baroness Warsi, he asked her to get to the bottom of what was blocking the school from getting through the process. The Baroness was also tasked with arranging for Cheron to meet a senior official at the Department for Education.

This turned out to be the only direct request made that day by Prime Minister David Cameron.

Things were beginning to change.

The case for a Christian-based school in Birmingham was growing into something that was more and more compelling.

# Preparation For The Fight

# Chapter One – Entrepreneur

*Three-six-nine,*
*The goose drank wine;*
*The monkey hung his knickers*
*On the washing line!*
*The line broke,*
*The monkey got choked,*
*And they all went to heaven*
*In a little row boat.*

The strange little rhyme sounded out from the Somerville Primary School playground. The girls stood in front of each other as they carried out their intricate clapping game to the sound of the rhyme. Look more closely and you will see Cheron organising the group.

If it wasn't the clapping game, skipping was the next best thing. Cheron and her school friends, Christine and Margaret, would spend most of their lunch times practising the complicated routines.

School was fun for the most part. So was home life.

Charles Road, Small Heath, Birmingham was home. A mid-terrace house painted white with a small walled garden at the front. Go around the back on most weekends and you'll see three small girls playing in the garden. Cheron is the middle child and does her best to keep an eye on younger sister Annette B. Big sister Audrey comes and goes, joining in with the activities when not helping Mum in the kitchen.

Today Annette B and Mary-Anne are getting a makeover. Mary-Anne is the doll, the proud possession of young Cheron. There's hair to comb and bathing is essential too. Cheron works intensely at the task as Mum looks on from the kitchen window.

Mum works as a nurse at the hospital and Dad at the local factory. Small Heath is a good place to grow up. South-east of Birmingham city centre, the community is a mix of Indian, Pakistani and West Indian alongside a historic white community. Birmingham City Football Club is not far away and draws a good number to the area on match days. Small Heath has a reasonable mix of housing too. Many, including Cheron's house, are Victorian properties, but there are lots of newer houses, plus a local business park.

For Cheron, born in Jamaica and moving to England during the Windrush period, whilst still a baby, this is home. She knows the streets and loves the people.

The Windrush connection is an important one. The SS *Empire Windrush* docked at Tilbury in 1948. The first of many ships, it carried immigrants from the West Indies, invited back to the 'Mother Country' to help rebuild after the ravages of war. But the promised welcome did not materialise. Most of the Windrush generation faced extreme racial injustice. A common sign in the windows of boarding houses for those early immigrants was 'No Blacks, No Irish, No Dogs.' Is it any surprise that Cheron and that next generation after Windrush have felt the need to respond to this injustice?

## Step of Faith

'Audrey, what did you do at church tonight?'

Cheron was curious to know why her big sister Audrey had held her hand up in church, indicating she wanted to become a Christian.

'I got saved, Cheron! That's what happened!'

'Saved? What's that?'

'At church – I prayed and asked Jesus to forgive me for all the wrong I had done and to be the Lord of my life. So now I'm saved and will go to heaven when I die.'

'Heaven? What's that? What do you mean?'

And so began Cheron's own faith journey. Audrey had found a genuine Christian faith, so Cheron copied her sister. Audrey got saved so Cheron wanted to get saved. Maybe not as dramatic as the Damascus Road experience but that would do for the time being.

Cheron's real moment of change came as a seven-year-old. Mum had a strong Christian faith and would regularly take the girls to church in Small Heath. It was there that Pastor Dennis and Sister Woodley helped Cheron join the dots . . . It wasn't enough to go to church. It wasn't enough to pray prayers. Jesus wanted a personal relationship with her. She prayed, asking God for forgiveness and to come into her life. He did. And to this day, that relationship with God is the most important thing in Cheron's life.

Baptised in water at the age of ten at Peel Street Church, Cheron considers her faith in Christ as the motivation for all she does.

And she does a lot!

## The Business

Enterprise came early.

Moving on from Somerville Primary School to Cockshut Hill Comprehensive in nearby Yardley at the age of twelve, Cheron noticed a gap in the business market.

Within the community, women's fashion not only involved clothes, but hair pieces too. These hair pieces, often worn by black women at weddings, parties, conventions and birthday celebrations, seemed to be very expensive. Surely there was a way of marketing something that was cheaper but still of a high quality?

And so began Cheron's first business. From her younger days in designing her sister Annette B's and her doll Mary-Anne's hair through to working as an apprentice hairdresser on Saturdays, her experiences helped in starting that very first business. In fact, Cheron's dad had noticed the way she had been styling Annette B's and Mary-Anne's hair and had joked to her that she would be a hairdresser. He did something about it too, getting Cheron that first apprenticeship at Chris's Hairdressing Salon, aged twelve.

Cheron's dad bought the weaving blocks for her to create the wefts and Chris taught Cheron how to use the wefts to make hairpieces. By the age of thirteen Cheron was successfully producing and selling high-end hair pieces for special occasions. It was all on a personal-recommendation basis and, much to her parent's delight, it meant that she never needed any pocket money growing up!

**I Am a Young Entrepreneur**
I am a young entrepreneur
I'm willing to take risks and do whatever it takes to succeed

I am a young entrepreneur
I conquer the market and I am the lion of the concrete jungle

I am a young entrepreneur
Any competition that comes my way sparks nothing but determination

I am a young entrepreneur
Dream big, passion gleaming
Creating, innovating – nonstop believing

I am a young entrepreneur
Making bold moves but always playing fair
The master of the market, always ready and prepared

I am a young entrepreneur
I fill gaps with products and services
That the modern market needs
Pushing future entrepreneurs
To do what they love and most importantly – succeed

I am a young entrepreneur
Primed for any obstacles that could come in my way
I overcome them with skill, precision and logic
Because that's what we do at King Solomon, the entrepreneurs of today

**Sofiat Majekodunmi & Afruika Ukaidi – Year 10 Students, King Solomon International Business School**

## Growing

Growing up came in two ways. Physically, of course, but also spiritually.

Cheron used to attend her church's national youth camps. For Cheron, these were a highlight of each year. Games, campfires, singing and plenty of food and Bible teaching. The annual camps became watershed moments for Cheron, building her faith and encouraging her in her own youth ministry.

Elder Gregory was Cheron's church pastor in those early years. To this day Cheron remembers his little sayings. He would approach the young Cheron who had inevitably been caught in some misdemeanour or other, bend down, look her in the eye and say something that always hit home.

'Sister Cheron, there is a fish that you should not buy, you should not sell, you should not eat, and you should not even give it away . . . it's called SELF FISH.'

And with a smile, he was gone to the next conversation and the next piece of wisdom.

## Learning

'Do you really think you'll make it?'

The sneer on his face said it all. Cheron's history teacher at Matthew Bolton College seemed to have the view that all children were doomed to fail, and he had Cheron particularly in his sights. The prediction was either a 'U' (unclassified) or an 'F' (fail) in A level history.

Cheron got an 'A' grade.

To this day, she uses the story as an illustration for young people as to what can be achieved and how to deal with the negative comments that come your way, ensuring that those comments never shape your future. It's something Cheron has had to learn again and again as the negative and disbelieving comments have been frequent and often, through the projects that she has pioneered.

Mr Smith, the A level English teacher was different. One conversation stands out in particular.

'So, Cheron, tell me, what university are you thinking of going to?'

'Pardon, sir?'

'What university will you apply for? What do you want to study?'

The questions were completely beyond Cheron's thinking. She'd never considered university at all. No one in her extended family, her church or local community had been to university. It was not something that she had contemplated. Cheron only knew of one or two friends from a distance who had taken that step.

Looking back, Mr Smith was being clever, of course, knowing full well Cheron had not considered it.

But with high-quality A levels under her belt, the conversation produced the fruit of a university place at Hull to study Social Studies. Though that didn't last long. Cheron realised that her real love was in the area of economics and she was able to change to a degree in Economic History. It was not just the economics that were an attraction. As Cheron says, 'History shapes the future. The more I know, the more I can shape it.'

## The Catalyst

It was during the second year of the degree that the lecturer came onto the scene. The name is long forgotten but the message is not. As Cheron sat there and the lecturer explained the business statistics in today's world, Cheron was horrified by the small number of black women who owned businesses.

She had intended to go into teaching or to work in the field of human resources once qualified, but that lecture was a catalyst for a change of direction.

As Cheron left the lecture theatre, she was in a deep conversation with a friend.

'I can't believe those statistics! So few women business owners and so few in senior business positions. Hardly a black woman in sight. I'm going to change that! I'm going to show that black women can make it in business.'

By the end of Cheron's university years, she had become so vocal about women in business that a lot of her friends were equally challenged.

Cheron put her teaching career and ambitions on hold to pursue her new-found passion for business. She followed up her degree with a specific business start-up course. Complete with business plan, Cheron then wanted someone to review and critique the plan, so she arranged for an interview with a local enterprise agency.

## The Agency

It didn't take Cheron long to explain her business plans to Christopher, the head of the Business Development Department, a commercial lawyer by profession. He was quiet for a while and then asked her a surprising question.

'Cheron, this is really impressive. Would you like to work here? Would you like a job at the agency?'

Cheron thought that the offer was for some sort of secretarial job. She had been trained as a secretary from an early age. Her mother had aspirations for her daughters to be office workers, not factory workers, so from age nine, Cheron, along with her sister Audrey, had been sent to Mrs Phipps, a woman who lived down the road, to be trained in shorthand and typing. But that's not want Cheron wanted to do.

'Do you mean working as a secretary, sir?'

'No, Cheron. That's not what I'm asking. Would you like to be a business advisor? I'd love you to join my team. You clearly have entrepreneurial skills, you are creative; I know you have great potential. I'd like to mentor you.'

A business advisor at the age of twenty-one. At the time, probably the youngest business advisor in the country. This was a sector full of older white men, not young black women. There was much to learn, and fast. The determination shown at university was finding its outlet in the business world.

Cheron had a large case load of business clients. The cases became progressively challenging as and when her line manager felt she was ready for the next step. By the age of twenty-two she was accompanying business clients to the bank to negotiate loans, negotiating with planning departments for planning permission, and liaising with lawyers on behalf of her clients. Upon meeting Cheron in person after dealing with her over the phone for a year or so, one of the lawyers was shocked to meet her. 'You're Cheron, the one that's been dealing with these big cases? But you're only a young girl!'

Cheron loved working at the agency, but there was still the long-term aim to work either in human resources management or in teaching, so whilst at the agency Cheron completed a master's in Human Resources as well as an Institute of Personnel and Development course. With these qualifications complete, and her ongoing passion for equality and justice, she started with a local authority in the Positive Action Unit, working in their human resources team.

She became disillusioned when it became very clear that the local authority lacked a real commitment towards equality. What was said was very different to what was done. The politically correct wording lacked any kind of follow through in practice. Cheron became disheartened and left both the local authority and the human resources profession after a couple of years, in favour of the business world where once trained, supported and empowered, people could take more control over their lives.

## A Quiet, Confident Leader

Her school teachers had consistently described Cheron in their reports as a quiet, confident leader. It's amazing how certain traits in children can be seen from an early age. Cheron was quiet, self-assured and a natural leader. She may not have been seen as a charismatic leader, but she was most certainly a dynamic one. Those traits, evident from an early age, were to become stronger over the years, enabling her to be courageous and resilient in the face of adversity.

Aged two, Cheron had already developed a strong sense of justice. Her four-year-old sister, Audrey, and a boy from the neighbourhood had been playing with Audrey's toys. The boy then stole Audrey's toys and ran out of the house leaving the front door open. Audrey sobbed uncontrollably. Cheron's dad grabbed his car keys and headed down the road to the boy's house. On his way he saw a little toddler running down the road after the boy with a stone in her hand. He was shocked when he realised it was his two-year-old Cheron. Justice was necessary and Cheron was leading on this. Her dad stopped the car, flung his arms around her whilst prizing the stone out of her hand, gently telling her that's not the way to do it. He scooped little Cheron up and together they continued on their journey in pursuit of justice. Justice was done.

By the age of twenty-nine, now an established business woman in her own rights, Cheron successfully secured the appointment as director for the Women's Business Development Agency for Coventry and Warwickshire. Justice outworked.

Shortly after being appointed, Cheron met the candidate that came a close second to her. The woman was dynamic, charismatic, highly educated, spoke nine languages, and had a strong business background. She was impressive. Cheron was baffled that the panel had chosen her over this candidate. She raised it with the chair.

'Cheron,' said the chair, 'you got the job because you were the best candidate. What pushed you over the line was your character. We felt we could trust you with a million pounds.'

Character. The agency was not a Christian organisation, neither were the panel Christians, but character was important to them. That word remained with Cheron for years. The word 'character' later found itself in the vision statement for the future school. Educational excellence and character development. Education is important, but character matters too.

Cheron's appointment wasn't without opposition though. Some complained about her age. And subtly, some complained about her colour.

Despite the challenges, Cheron was highly successful in her job. She was elected for five consecutive years as chair of the National Women's Business Development Network. She loved that role as she was able to make a genuine difference to women's businesses on a national scale. She initiated many innovative projects and hosted the first ever national business women's exhibition at the prestigious National Exhibition Centre. Patricia Hewitt, the Secretary of State for Trade and Industry at the time, speaking at the event, described Cheron's agency as the most successful of its kind in the country.

**The Visible Business Woman**

No longer will she remain invisible
No longer will they pass her by
No longer will she be considered dispensable
For now she is being recognised

There's so many business women that could pick up this top award
As the ability to balance work and home is something we must applaud
Such skill, such talent, such enthusiasm
Such commitment, determination, such dynamism.

And no, she's not doing things any differently
from the way she's always done
But they stand respectfully
in awe of the prize she has won

It's not only the money or the trophy that's presented on the night
that makes her jump for joy and brings her great delight
but the fact that she can stand with dignity
and claim victory over the battle of invisibility

We say goodbye to the invisible woman
no longer will she be unseen anymore
We say hello to all enterprising women
as they push open the visible door

**Written by Staff at the Women's Business Development Agency,
1999**

By now Cheron, adding to her qualifications, had completed a master's in Business Administration and secured a distinction. Whilst at university she won the Royal Mail Prize for Marketing Student of the Year.

The hard work was opening further doors. She was getting noticed in the business world. Wolverhampton University took an interest and appointed her as a senior leader in the Office for External Development, with responsibilities for the university's business development, enterprise, careers, employer liaison and funding. Her appointment was a baptism by fire. Within an hour of starting her job she was informed that as the most senior person in the department, she was officially the deputy director.

'And by the way,' said a colleague, 'the director is leaving.'

Within a matter of weeks Cheron, based at Wolverhampton Science Park, was leading a very large and complex department.

She was fortunate to have the Pro Vice-Chancellor, Professor Gerald Bennett, as her line manager. From what may be viewed as a white and middle-class background, he nevertheless had an acute awareness of the challenges Cheron was to face.

'Cheron, you're the first black woman this university has appointed to a senior leadership role. It will be tough. You've got to be thick skinned to survive, but I'm here for you.'

There were many challenges, but Cheron's annual appraisals were such an affirming experience for her. Professor Bennett, always supportive, recorded what he saw as first-class leadership.

Cheron was excited about being able to lead the development of the university's student and graduate enterprise services. She employed a dynamic team of business practitioners to work in the newly established unit at the science park, providing business advice, training and support to student and graduate entrepreneurs. She played a key role in enabling the university to secure a £2m grant to develop business incubation facilities and she worked alongside the academic staff in Wolverhampton Business School in promoting an exciting new master's degree.

The work was pressured but Cheron loved every moment. This was what she had been born for. Her entrepreneurial skills came to the fore. Her leadership was on show. And she was pioneering in a predominantly white and male world.

Then came the leaflet.

# Chapter Two – Black Boys Can

It was just an A5 printed leaflet. Cheron had picked it up on her travels as the title had caught her attention. It was offering funding for charities working in the area of education.

## Self fish

There was no real relevance to the day job, but the leaflet went into the handbag rather than into the bin. Cheron thought that maybe it would be of interest to her church. The church was not doing a great deal at the time with the youth in the area and maybe the charity funding could spark something off.

Remembering the old saying of Elder Gregory about the 'self fish', Cheron thought to herself, 'Well, I don't really need this, but it could help others.'

She called a meeting with her sister Audrey, a qualified accountant, together with some of her peers from church to discuss it. Along with Audrey were Clive Bailey, an international business professional, and Michael Bailey, a social worker.

The four of them gathered at Cheron's home. Refreshments were served. The traditional Jamaican bun and cheese with cans of ginger beer. Then the leaflet came out of the handbag.

'I just wonder whether there is an opportunity for us here. It's real funding and could meet a real need. Just look around you at the housing estates. There are so many children and young people out on the streets, getting into trouble. Do you think we could do something? Maybe a children's club or something?'

'The real need is among black boys,' said Michael. 'I see it all the time. Too many of them are underachieving. They get told that they will achieve nothing, so many of them live up to it. There are so many hanging around on street corners right through the school holidays. What about a black boys' club? Something that gets them together? Something that tells them they can succeed?'

Michael's comments made so much sense. By the end of the meeting, there was an outline plan.

The intention was to set up an educational club, a six-week summer programme, especially aimed at the black boys out on the streets. Michael, with a spark of inspiration, came up with the name 'Black Boys Can'. It was just perfect. It was a deliberate rebuke to the many who were critical of black youth, suggesting that most black boys would never make anything of themselves and would end up in gangs and crime.

It didn't have to be that way and the club would gather them together and inspire them. The intention would be to encourage and to clearly state that they could make something of their lives. They didn't need to be a statistic.

Empowering lives through education, training and development has remained central to all of the charity's successive ventures.

The funding application went in, but after the second round of reviews, they failed in the bid. However, by then things were moving at quite a pace. The planners decided to go ahead anyway. They sought help from the church and friends and were able to gather around £200. This was a far cry from the potential £10,000 that had been on offer through the charity application, but it was enough to open the doors at least. It was a mustard seed.

## Off the Streets

As Cheron walked from the car, she saw a group of boys she knew well, hanging around outside the building.

'Are you boys coming in? We'll be starting in a few minutes.'

Silence.

Looks of disinterest.

'Come on! You really should! I'm sure you're going to enjoy it.'

They came in and hung around at the back. One of them, James Nolan, was particularly uninterested. He had spent the last two weeks trying to persuade all the boys he knew to boycott the programme, so Cheron was surprised to see him there at all. His parents had insisted he come.

Later that week, Cheron met James and his parents. Mum and Dad knew James was challenging, and had sent him to a supplementary school, but to no avail. Black Boys Can was their last hope. However, there was no apparent change in attitude.

Week two followed a similar course. Cheron had arranged for a guest speaker, talking of how to find your sweet spot in terms of future business.

Still no engagement. Clear eye-avoidance. And a swift exit as soon as the session ended.

Week three saw a small change. Despite himself, James was caught up by the speaker, Paul Street. It was a dynamic session and his stories of achieving in various industries caught the imagination of the boys attending.

By week four, James was not only on time but sitting near the front. His story is the story of many black boys. Their default position is one of failure but as they receive encouragement, they blossom. They become excited with prospects and opportunities they were not previously aware of.

James's story didn't end there. His school work picked up to such an extent that he received a school award for being a top-ten most-improved student. He became a helper at the club. He designed the Black Boys Can logo, the basis of which is still incorporated into today's design.

As the six-week course came to an end, it was clear to the team that they had hit on something that had worked. The boys wanted to be there. They enjoyed the challenge and responded positively. Even outside of club times, behaviour was different. The boys were more engaged in life – there was less hanging around on street corners.

One of the trainers had spoken so powerfully about the power of love that one of the boys came up with the catch phrase 'Love is a weapon' and then a rhyme:

*Love is a weapon, use it to overcome hatred, defend and attack,*

*Use it even when your enemies talk ill of you behind your back*

*Use it to do good to them that hurt you*

*Even when their evil deeds are in full view*

*When they do you wrong*

*Remember that by blessing them you will become strong*

*(Used with permission from Black Boys Can, Acocks Green)*

Spoken in conversations, shouted on the streets, love was indeed winning a battle.

## The Can-Do Culture

The team had a success on their hands. The boys did not want the programme to end; they begged the team to continue with the project. Black Boys Can had only been intended for six weeks.

But there was no doubt about it, it was a triumph and needed to continue. During the holidays, it had been running as a three-days-a-week club, but now with a return to school, it became a Saturday club.

The team made sure that the same high quality was maintained. The various speakers gave of their time and energy for free, as did the team.

Black Boys Can was so successful, it began to be talked of further afield. And that's when it came to the attention of the press, including, remarkably, the *Times Educational Supplement*. A journalist arrived to interview the volunteers and some of the boys. The following week Black Boys Can was the front-page story in the *Times Educational Supplement*, headlined as 'The Can-Do Culture'.

For the next couple of weeks, the phone didn't stop ringing. Calls were coming in from all over the country – from parents, from teachers, from headteachers – all of them asking the same thing: 'Could you please set up a Black Boys Can project for us?' Needless to say, the team were nowhere near ready for that.

## A Black Boys Can student . . . 15 years on

Society always portrayed black boys as underachievers. My mother, a single parent, was determined I would not be just another statistic, another black boy who underachieved.

I was diagnosed as having a special educational need so had additional challenges to overcome. So when she heard of the Black Boys Can project, that was it, I had to enrol, whether I wanted to or not. I was twelve years old at the time.

Black Boys Can made all the difference to my life.

It provided me with invaluable skills and experiences that supplemented my academic studies and gave me a sense of purpose, confidence and most importantly developed my character.

It wasn't until I was at university that I was diagnosed as having a further special educational need. I don't know where I would be today if Black Boys Can wasn't there for me during my schooling years, helping me to develop skills to compensate for my special educational needs.

Their residential programmes, career fairs, gala dinner awards events, national conferences and Excell3's Amos Bursary Scheme provided me with life-changing opportunities.

When society said I can't, Black Boys Can said you can. So I did. When society presents the statistics that say black men are more likely to end up in prison than go to university, Black Boys Can steered me away from trouble, away from prison. I did go to university and graduated with a 2:1.

When society gives up on black boys who don't grow up with a father, Black Boys Can didn't, and they surrounded me with positive black male role models.

Although society portrays black men as drug dealers and robbers, Black Boys Can taught me not to be defined by society. I am a law-abiding citizen, a married man, and a successful business owner.

Never in my wildest dreams did I envisage that one day I would be on the management committee for Black Boys Can, providing similar opportunities I received from the project to the next generation of black boys.

**Xavier Hamilton**

## Rising to the Challenge

'What are we going to do, Cheron?'

Audrey, Michael and Clive were concerned. The calls kept coming. People were asking for meetings. The team needed to decide whether they were going to say 'sorry, we can't help' or rise to the challenge.

They decided to rise to the challenge.

They went about setting up a charity, a company and an innovative community franchise model. Further development saw a legal agreement and a community franchise pack including all the necessary material and processes to get going. Eventually around twenty different Black Boys Can projects were running in different parts of the country: Birmingham, London, Liverpool, Derby, Bristol, and many more. Each one happened independently, linked in through the franchise. From a humble beginning with just twenty boys, the project grew to reach thousands of boys around the country.

Dr Trevor Adams from Luton was one of the instigators of the first community franchise project to get started. In one of his interviews, he articulated his views about the project:

'Black Boys Can is not only our inspirational name and belief, but it is also the positive claim that we make about black boys. Underpinning this claim is our belief that black boys, like other children, are gifted and talented. We believe that they are born with the innate capacity for growth. We also believe that adopting a holistic approach in working positively with black boys, their families and community provides them with the right support. It enables them to unleash their potential to achieve and excel. Time and time again, over the last twenty-one years throughout the country, we have seen our claim substantiated. The high performances of black boys within our practices provides the evidence that Black Boys Can.'

When Cheron met the then parliamentary opposition leader, he was impressed with how Black Boys Can was innovatively applying a commercial franchising concept to benefit socially. The concept, also now known as social franchising, began to spread throughout the country.

## Patron

From the start, Audrey was on the lookout for a patron for the project.

She attended an event where Lord Bill Morris was the keynote speaker. Lord Morris was the General Secretary of the Transport and General Workers' Union. An exceptional leader, he was the first black leader of a major British trade union. Audrey was convinced that he would be an ideal patron for Black Boys Can. She approached him, not really expecting to get a positive response. But she did.

He was sold on the concept of empowering black boys and became the patron. He had strong values and was uncompromising in his belief and promotion of dignity, fairness and equality. A real role model for black boys, he gave his time, sound advice, attended all major events, and was actively involved in lobbying for change for black boys.

## Oxford

Cheron became intrigued by disadvantaged children, particularly black boys, who had succeeded academically against the odds. How did they do it? Very little was known about the success factors as research studies tended to focus on their underachievement. The idea of researching this appealed to Cheron. She toyed with the notion and shared this with Audrey.

'Go to Oxford.'

'Oxford? Audrey, that's not a university I've even considered.'

'Well you should. I'm sure you'll meet their criteria. You're a high achiever, surely that will put you in good stead for Oxford. Go for it, Cheron.'

Cheron bolstered up the courage to ring Oxford University to make a tentative enquiry. Whilst waiting for the phone to answer she heard, in her head, a loud antagonistic voice speaking in the Jamaican Patois dialect, saying, 'What a way fe you ches high.' When interpreted into English this means, 'Who do you think you are? You're going way above your station.'

Cheron was just about to put down the phone when the receptionist answered. There was no going back. She applied.

She prayed to God and promised herself that if she got through to Oxford she would open the doors for black boys and other under-represented groups of young people to gain similar access to Oxford.

She was invited for an interview. It was hard. One of the professors had seemingly written her off before they started. The panel came up with all sorts of reasons why they shouldn't offer her a place.

'We don't offer many part-time doctorates in the Department for Education, in fact we are only going to offer two this year.'

'Doing a doctorate at Oxford is hard work; it's very demanding here. Our standards are high; we are unlikely to find you a supervisor for this year.'

'You're working full-time and running a national educational charity at the same time. We can't see how you can do it.'

The chair of the panel had kept quiet whilst the debate went on, then when they had finished, he spoke.

'I think she can.'

All eyes turned towards Professor Geoffrey Walford.

'Yes, I believe she can. She has strong academic credentials, three good degrees, two master's including an MBA with distinction. And achieving an MBA through distance learning isn't the easy option. She has glowing references. I believe she can do it.'

'Yes, but who is this Professor Johnson who has given the reference? Is he honest enough?'

'Yes, he is,' said Professor Walford. 'I know him personally. I worked with him for years.'

Cheron was through. The highly renowned international Professor Geoffrey Walford chose Cheron to be one of his doctoral students. Only the best would do.

She started the doctorate, but from time to time kept thinking about the promise she had made to herself to open doors for black boys and others to get through to Oxford University. She didn't know how this could be done, but as the doctorate would take six to eight years, she had time to figure out how best to do it. Cheron prayed about it and trusted God that it would happen.

It didn't take six to eight years for the doors to open.

Cheron was still in her first year at Oxford when, during a meeting with a professor, she mentioned Black Boys Can and her role in it. The professor was fascinated and wanted to know more. At the end of their meeting the professor said, 'This university would love to know about your project.' She asked Cheron to wait a minute whilst she made a telephone call.

Within minutes, Cheron was walking through the streets of Oxford with the professor to be introduced to the head of the Widening Participation Department. The head gathered the staff together to listen to what Cheron had to say. Cheron felt totally unprepared. She had no speech ready, no PowerPoint presentation to use, no promotional material to distribute. Yet here she was making a presentation to a room full of Oxford staff.

They were sold. They wanted a Black Boys Can project at Oxford. By the end of her first year, a project had been launched, and two years later the WISE and Apex programmes, bringing hundreds of disadvantaged students into Oxford was underway. Many black boys subsequently obtained bachelor's degrees, master's and doctorates from Oxford.

## Divinely Orchestrated Encounters

Cheron's doctorate at Oxford was an international research study. This took her to the USA.

For the research, she needed to gain access to key members of staff and students at the University of Harvard and the University of Central Florida. She tried. She got so far, then all the leads dried up. Determined as she was, Cheron decided to board the aeroplane and head towards the University of Central Florida anyway, hoping that somehow the doors would be opened.

Whilst on the campus she asked for directions for the student union. The man she had asked looked at her in a quizzical manner.

'Er, excuse me, but are you Cheron?'

Taken aback, Cheron replied that she was.

'I'm Delaney. You emailed me several months ago. So sorry I didn't get back to you, but . . .'

Cheron couldn't believe she was talking to the very person she had been trying to contact from England. Delaney opened the doors Cheron needed to conduct her research at the University of Florida. Once again, persistence and prayer had opened a door – in this case a God-instance on the university campus. What are the odds of the one person Cheron needed to meet out of a student population of 70,000 and 12,000 staff, being the one she approached for directions?

A year later, Cheron caught the plane to Harvard University, hoping to gain access in the same way as she had done in Florida. But there was to be severe disappointment as she reached the entrance to Harvard. The university campus was not accessible to the general public. Cheron couldn't believe she had travelled all the way to the United States in vain. What to do? In need of thought as well as sustenance, she headed to a nearby shop in order to buy one of her favourite comfort foods, a Galaxy milk chocolate bar. On her way out of the shop, she asked a man if he had any contacts within Harvard University. He said yes. She briefly explained why she needed to gain access. Then the man looked at her in a quizzical manner.

'Are you from England?'

'Yes.'

'I'm Roger, Roger Bond. You emailed me some months ago.'

'You're Roger? I'm Cheron!'

'I'm so sorry I didn't get back to you, but . . .'

Hard to believe.

Out of a student population of over 22,000 at Harvard and 13,000 staff, Cheron had bumped into the individual she had been trying to make contact with all those months ago.

God is amazing.

With the new-found knowledge gained through the time she spent at Harvard and Central Florida, this not only contributed to her doctorate but also influenced the positive action work she continued to pursue in subsequent years.

## Gratitude

Back in the UK, the Black Boys Can programme continued to grow. Cheron always advised new staff during their induction not to expect any gratitude from the boys on the programme; this was something that may come later on in their lives, she would counsel.

How wrong could she be.

Neil, a Year 10 boy, after the first day on the Oxford University Black Boys Can programme, came over to her. Somewhat shyly, he said:

'Miss Cheron, thanks for organising this programme for us.'

And with that, he was gone. Such a simple thing, but Cheron was taken aback. It meant so much to her.

Neil became the first Black Boys Can student to secure a place at Oxford University. That same year the Prime Minster was challenging Oxford and Cambridge to be more proactive in increasing their numbers of black students. He had noted that in the last year Oxford had only admitted one African Caribbean black male student. That one African Caribbean boy was a Black Boys Can student. Neil. The young man with a heart of gratitude.

## Active

Cheron became very active at Oxford, but not in typical ways.

She was invited to join staff on a working party at Oxford, chaired by a vice chancellor. The working party, amongst other things, reviewed Oxford's equal opportunities policy and access policies and practice, with a view to removing unnecessary barriers to access for less advantaged students. Cheron was able to share the knowledge she had gained during the time she had spent with staff at Florida and Harvard.

Cheron was also invited to speak at one of Oxford's national widening participation conferences attended by most of the universities in the country.

Her amazing years at Oxford culminated in the launch of her first book. She felt honoured that one of Oxford's vice chancellors chaired the event and that David Lammy MP, then Minster for Higher Education, was the keynote speaker. Her supervisor Professor Geoffrey Walford was proud of his student. Not only had she completed her doctorate in record time but her external examiner from King's College London was so impressed with Cheron that she invited her to be a keynote speaker at a book launch event at King's College London. Professor Walford had taken a gamble on her. It had paid off. He said she could. And Cheron did.

## Excell3

Excell3 became the name for Cheron's work. It aimed to transform lives through three initiatives: education, training and development. The charity has continued to expand. They began forming partnerships with a range of universities. Baroness Amos and her sister Colleen Amos approached Excell3 to become the parent charity for the Amos Bursary. Excell3 fulfilled that role for ten years until the bursary was in a position to set up their own charity.

Excell3 contributed to a number of grassroots and government publications, participating in various government think-tanks, as well as attending the Queen's garden party, the Prime Minister's reception at 10 Downing Street and the Chancellor of the Exchequer's reception at No 11. The charity presented to nearly 100 MPs at a cross-party event hosted for them at the House of Lords.

It was at one of these events at the House of Lords that Cheron met Margaret Thatcher, the longest-serving British Prime Minister of the 20th century, and the first woman to hold that office. Cheron had expected to meet the good and the great at these events, but she didn't expect Margaret Thatcher to have taken such an interest in her. In fact, whilst talking with Cheron she grabbed her hand and asked for a photo shoot.

As a child Cheron used to join in with her school friends chanting 'Margaret Thatcher the milk snatcher!' – a reference to her decision to remove free school milk whilst holding the position of Education Minister. Never in her wildest dreams did Cheron envisage that one day Margaret Thatcher would be snatching her hand at the House of Lords.

## Academy Sponsor

Success led to further success. Cheron was getting noticed. Her high-energy approach was creating a high profile too, so when the opportunity to sponsor an academy came along and she applied, she was welcomed by the authorities.

It seemed a natural move for Excell3 to sponsor a school. With a good track record already, it would be easy to step into this new arena.

Nothing could be further from the truth.

# The Fight To Become An Academy Sponsor

# Chapter Three – Starting The Fight

'What did you just say?'

Cheron was at the wheel of the car, accompanied by some of her Excell3 staff.

'I was just saying,' said Stephen, 'did you see the new government initiative for school sponsorship? They are inviting businesses to sponsor schools, and one of the responses is a Christian car dealership that's planning to start work with some schools in the north of England.'

The car journey to an Excell3 event in Derby was a bit of a blur after that for Cheron. She had started to think . . . and to plan.

Why not? Why not Excell3? If a car dealership can do it, then why not our educational charity? After all, the stated vision of the charity was 'transforming lives through education, training and development'. That fitted in exactly with the new government plans.

The very next morning, Cheron called together her Excell3 board. Clive Bailey recalls the excitement and determination on Cheron's face. Even though she had heard of it just the day before, preliminary plans had been prepared overnight and were presented for a potential project.

'It's a big ask, I know it is,' said Cheron, 'but we can do this. I want us to go for it!'

An hour later, Clive and the whole board were agreed, initial strategies prepared. And a journey had begun.

## Approaches

But how to get started? Who to contact? How receptive would the establishment be to a black majority led charity being an academy sponsor in any case?

Cheron approached Birmingham City Council in order to establish whether it was possible for Excell3 to sponsor a school in their locality. A few phone calls later found Cheron and board member Henroy Green outside the offices of the Birmingham Director of Education. It was a warm day and both were concerned to look as cool as possible.

'The director will see you now.'

With the pleasantries over, Cheron began to tell her story, her passion for education and all that had been achieved through the charity so far.

The director didn't say much at first and it was hard to guess how engaged he was with the presentation.

They needn't have worried.

'Cheron, Henroy, this is really exciting! At present all the businesses that have expressed an interest in our schools are based in London. But you are local. Not only that, you have such relevant experience.'

And with that, the coffee cups were cleared, and a map placed on the table.

'Our Building Schools for the Future programme has a budget of £750 million all told. We have eight schools that are looking for the new academy status. Five have been pencilled in with other sponsors. These are the three schools we still have available for sponsorship . . .'

One of those schools stood out above the rest. College High School was in Erdington, not too far from Excell3's offices. Things were fitting into place.

The director advised Cheron to make a formal application to become an academy sponsor. She rose to the challenge. An initial application to the Department for Education was sent in and initial approval was given in 2008. The application was particularly welcomed by the Department for Education as Cheron would be the first female and black academy sponsor in the country; a tick in the equalities box much needed by the government.

Lord Bill Morris, Excell3's patron, was able to lend support, not least because he was also Chancellor of Staffordshire University. His university link meant that Staffordshire University, and in particular the Business Studies Department, became a formal education partner with Excell3. This link to the university provided a significant amount of kudos to their application.

There was more good news. The council invited Excell3 to become partners with all the other Birmingham academies, recognising their relevance and experience.

## Resources

The challenges ahead of the charity were considerable, not least the two million pounds required to sponsor the school. However, the first stages required only a five-hundred-pound deposit. The deposit was raised in just three weeks and Cheron was ready with a plan for the remaining amount.

Resources of a different kind were needed too. There was no doubt that the form-filling and the meeting-attending needed to get this off the ground would be a strain on the charity. It meant diverting staff away from other projects and sacrificing time scales on other undertakings.

But it would be worth it. To be able to sponsor a Birmingham school. To be able to see Christians from all denominations united as one, focusing on what they have in common rather than majoring on their differences. To see young people develop an enterprising mind-set. To be able to replicate the success of Black Boys Can to help disadvantaged children, transforming and fulfilling their potential. To be able to replicate the success of Excell3 on such a broader field. All these reasons and more meant that the time, energy and money required was more than worthwhile.

## The Phone Call

'Hello, Doctor Byfield? This is the office of the Director of Education. We have had some additional interest in the sponsorship of College High. Please could you get back to us?'

Cheron called back later the same day. It appeared that an offer had come in from a Muslim businessman, a member of the House of Lords.

He wanted to join Excell3 as a co-sponsor, with 50 per cent each in terms of investment.

This created a dilemma for the board as it was essential from their point of view that the school had a Christian ethos. They communicated this via the Director of Education's office and suggested meeting with the Lord to discuss it at the forthcoming tour of the school premises.

In the meantime, Excell3 went the extra mile, preparing a paper for consideration by College High, which set out the vision for the school. The paper was clear and thorough. It was sent to Birmingham Education Department to be forwarded to the school. Unknown to Cheron at the time, the school never saw it.

## The Visit

It was with some excitement that Cheron, Stephen Brooks and Henroy Green travelled over to College High. They were introduced to the headteacher, Mrs Popratnjak. The relationship that started that day with Mrs Popratnjak would reap rewards further on in this story as she became involved in the leadership at the future school.

But meeting Mrs Popratnjak was one of the very few plus-points from that day. The team were expecting to be able to have time with the Lord but, after the formal handshakes, he and his team were taken on a separate tour of the school. What concerned Cheron and her team was that the local authority representative, the head and the senior team all went on that tour. Cheron and her colleagues were left with what was very clearly a 'second tier' school team.

The tour was formal and brief.

Something was wrong. Cheron could tell that much.

The truth came out a few days later.

## Dropped

'Doctor Byfield? I have the Director of Education on the phone.'

It was a short phone call. Excell3 had been dropped as sponsors and College High was given entirely to the Lord, the London sponsor.

Cheron's hand remained fixed to the receiver. Slowly she replaced it in its cradle. What had just happened? She felt physically sick. Overcome with emotion, Cheron leaned back in her chair. Feeling close to tears, she cried out in prayer. Surely this could not be happening. All that work. All that time.

The council told the press that 'The school in question has been waiting some time for sponsor arrangements to be put in place and there is an urgent need for a speedy resolution. The decision was therefore made that this particular opportunity for sponsorship will be apportioned elsewhere to ensure current required timescales be met.'

Required timescales? What timescales? Nothing could be further from the truth. The council knew that they had raised the required money to proceed, and in just three weeks. The team felt it was unjust and lacked integrity.

They were devastated. It seemed so unfair. All that effort, blown away in a one-minute phone call.

The Lord, a Life Peer, was no doubt an exceptional businessman but his organisation was already sponsoring two other Birmingham schools. So why give him a third one? The idea of sponsored academies was still new, so he, like so many of the academy sponsors in those early days, had no track record he could point to and, on a number of measures, Excell3 was by far the more experienced potential sponsor for this project.

It was hard to pick the team up. It was hard for Cheron to pick herself up from the upsetting news.

What had they done wrong? Nothing. All forms had been completed. All applications had been successful. All hurdles had been leapt over.

Had there been some internal politics between the Department for Education and the Lord? What had been said? What had been promised? Was this some form of racism or religious discrimination because they were Christians?

It simply wasn't right.

## Stand Up for Justice

There was only ever one man who showed true justice on this Earth,
His name was Jesus Christ; sent to us by virgin birth.

His example, revealed through Holy Scripture is for you and me,
We must follow daily in His way and act with integrity.

Love your neighbour as yourself and pray for those who hurt you.
With all your heart, soul, mind and strength love our Saviour too.

Justice is doing good even in the face of adversity,
For as we act with justice, we will grow in unity.

Remember the sacrifice Jesus made when He died upon the tree?
No one said that standing up for justice was meant to be easy.

So never tire of doing good, and act justly every day.
Stand against oppression and follow in His way.

Bring justice to the fatherless and plead the widow's cause.
Walk humbly with your God and true treasure you will store.

**Mrs Holdsworth – Primary Teacher, King Solomon International
Business School**

## The Protests

By this stage there were a lot of supporters backing Excell3. Churches
had been praying for the project. Many in education had given their
support. Mentors. Supporters. Financial backers. Parents of potential
pupils. All were outraged.

A meeting was called. In fact, this developed into a number of
consultation meetings. In addition to the supporters and parents, a few
political radicals attended, including the well-known activist Beanie
Brown. Some of those attending these first meetings were very keen for
action. They wanted to 'burn down Babylon', destroy the corrupt and
oppressive forces in pursuit of freedom.

There was a proposal to stage a march with placards, ending at the
Birmingham education offices. Others wanted to utilise their contacts
with the press to expose the corruption.

Cheron and Clive weren't quite so sure about these actions and
successfully persuaded the protesters to hold off for the time being.
Cheron was aware that the Department for Education were embarrassed
by what had happened and she felt that a more peaceful approach was
more appropriate.

Further meetings followed, including one that was particularly well attended at Aston University. The leader of the council was invited but declined. He did, however, send a representative.

The representative caught the mood of the meeting. He saw the passion and the support and went away with a positive view of the team. He gave an assurance that the local authority would support a further bid.

Unfortunately, this didn't happen. The immediate response to the protest meetings was positive but as time went on, things became less encouraging. Birmingham City Council had initially apologised and promised another school. But the final school in the academy process dropped out, so the promise was withdrawn. There simply wasn't a school to offer to Excell3.

There was enough of a public outcry for the whole matter to reach the ears of Lord Adonis, the Undersecretary of State for Schools. He invited Excell3 and representatives of Birmingham Council, including the leader of the council, to a meeting in London. Cheron and Stephen went, along with Lord Bill Morris, their patron. Bishop Wilton Powell the National Overseer for the Church of God of Prophecy also attended.

The council did not turn up for the meeting. They apologised and said that they thought the meeting was in Birmingham.

It was clear to all, including Lord Adonis, that the council were playing politics.

The team were angry. They had spent hours preparing bids, answering questions and filling forms. It appeared that the council could then simply turn around and shrug their shoulders; failing to accept any responsibility for the broken promises and non-attended meetings was unacceptable.

The ongoing protest meetings began to receive some publicity so that by the time Lord Adonis was due in Birmingham to announce the launch of the Birmingham academy programme sponsors, there was more than a little nervousness in the corridors of power as to what kind of welcome he would receive.

And before the formal event from the Department for Education, Cheron had one more protest meeting to attend. Unlike earlier ones, the press appeared interested. The story was getting out. Just a few days before the formal unveiling of the sponsors, this was not what the government wanted.

## The Pressure

On the day of the final consultation meeting, the phone calls started to arrive. Cheron was in her office when the first one came through.

'Hi, Cheron, I've got the leader of the council on the line for you.'

What followed was a bit of a sob-story. A fulsome apology for the way the council had acted with regard to College High and a promise to find another school.

'If only you had picked up the phone to me, Cheron, this wouldn't have happened. But please could you and your team make sure that today's meeting goes ahead without public protest and journalists?'

As far as Cheron was aware, there were to be no formal protests. They had encouraged the activists to stand down for now and this final event was to be more of a planning meeting for the next steps.

Nevertheless, it was a welcome call – the council were clearly aware of the underhand way in which they had treated Excell3 and the leader of the council seemed keen to put it right.

Phone calls from Lord Adonis' office, came next. Then one from Lord Bill Morris. As a patron to the charity, he too had received a call, this one directly from Lord Adonis. The flavour of each call was the same. 'Keep your people in order and we will meet your concerns.'

By this time, Cheron was feeling nervous. Why all this interest? Sure, the meeting might embarrass the government if the protestors' stories were repeated in the press, but was that such a bad thing? Why was she receiving so many calls? Clearly someone in government was 'spooked' by the idea of the meeting. But it seemed to be a bit of an over-the-top response to just one meeting.

The stakes got higher still. In the afternoon a call came in directly from Iain Duncan-Smith, former opposition leader for the Conservative Party.

Then more calls from local counsellors, some calling more than once. The council wanted supporters to boycott the meeting. Some of the supporters said that they, too, had been contacted by the council and encouraged not to attend the meeting that evening.

The pressure was intense. With every phone call, Cheron felt more and more weighed down by the whole thing. She was stressed. She couldn't think straight.

And then, when she tried to get up from her desk – she couldn't move. Literally. Cheron had lost all feeling from her waist down. She could not move her legs.

Panic set in. Cheron had to be at the meeting that evening. She had to keep an eye on the activists. She had to respond to the phone calls that day. What was she to do?

Her heart beating fast, Cheron tried to move again. Nothing. A silent scream. She simply could not move. The stress of it all had led her body into a state of paralysis.

'Lord, help me. Please help.'

## The Prayer

No sooner had the prayer gone up than another phone call came in.

But this one was different.

'Hi, Cheron, it's Reverend Nims here. Do you remember me? We met at a conference some time ago.'

Reverend Nims Obunge is the CEO of the Peace Alliance. He works as a faith and community leader, particularly in the area of justice, equality and social cohesion. News of the unrest had spread across the country.

'Oh, hi, Reverend. Yes, I remember.'

'Cheron, please excuse the interruption, but I've heard about the turmoil regarding the academy in Birmingham. The news has reached London. I've been praying for you. I feel God wants you to know this – you will have a school in Birmingham. I believe God has decreed it and nothing is going to stop it. Just as Israel went into the land of Canaan, so will you. You are going to eat the fruit of the land. God has decreed it!'

'Oh wow. Reverend Nims, I don't know what to say. Thank you so much. You have no idea what this means, on today of all days.'

Cheron went on to tell Reverend Nims about the final protest meeting scheduled that night and the numerous calls she had received from government offices as well as the council asking her to control the protesters.

'Pastor, it has all got a bit much. I think I'm in shock and suffering from paralysis. I can't move. I've lost all feeling below my waist. I'm not sure what's happened.'

Reverend Nims listened and then said, 'I'm going to pray over the phone, Cheron, pray for you right now.'

What followed was the most beautiful and powerful prayer of healing and release.

By the time Reverend Nims had finished praying, Cheron was completely healed. All the feeling came back and she was able to stand and walk as if nothing had happened.

On a day of intense pressure, at a moment when even Cheron's body was giving up, God sent the right man with the right phone call. Not even a close friend, but the right minister from London with God's word and God's authority to release the situation.

In case Cheron had forgotten, God wanted her to know one thing. He was in control.

# Chapter Four – Politics And Pressure

After all the phone calls and the stress of the day, the meeting was a welcome relief! Cheron arrived early at Birmingham University, the venue for the meeting, and by the time it started there were around 250 people present.

There was definitely a sense of betrayal and a desire to push through, to challenge the council with the underhanded way they had managed the process. But the speeches were sincere and polite.

First up was Henroy Green, one of the Excell3 board members. He related the journey, the promises and the disappointments.

'If Birmingham was not our home city, we would simply walk away from what we feel to be this unjust situation, but Birmingham *is* our home city. We fight on.'

Then the microphone was given to Indrajit Bhogal, a keen supporter of Excell3. Indrajit had conducted her own investigations as to how things had transpired:

'The council advised that they needed more time to discuss with Excell3 the details of the funders and partners to ensure they share common values. This appears to have been a mere excuse for taking the decision to give the school to another organisation, as the funders and partners would have been prepared to meet with the council immediately – and in any case they were only ever a telephone call away.

'As an independent person I am concerned about the process that was followed, or indeed lack of process, by the city council in deciding to retract on its agreement with Excell3 to sponsor the allocated school. I feel the whole matter is totally unacceptable – there are so many questions which must be answered.

'Why have Birmingham schools been outsourced to London companies? Why did Birmingham's Local Authority Education Scrutiny

Committee not even know that Excell3 had bid for a school? Is it because the council is anti community-led academies? Is it because the council is anti Christian-led academies? Is it because the council is anti black-led academies?'

## Another Offer

The launch event in Birmingham for the first tranche of academies was well attended. Lord Adonis was the guest of honour. He still wanted Cheron to attend and she accepted the invitation. As Lord Adonis got up to speak, he looked over the audience and his eyes came to rest on Cheron. It was clear he had singled her out. Not hard to spot as the only black woman there and perhaps her presence gave him the assurance that there would be no trouble from those still upset by the poor behaviour of Birmingham Council.

He needn't have worried. It is never Cheron's intention to cause trouble. She did manage a brief conversation with Lord Adonis after the event. He again apologised and promised he would be in touch.

True to his word, an invitation arrived for a meeting at his offices in London. Cheron went along with Lord Bill Morris and Bishop Wilton Powell. At the meeting Lord Adonis recognised the inappropriate practices at Birmingham Council and pledged his commitment to find another school for sponsorship.

Shortly afterwards, the Life Peer who was given the school that had initially been allocated to Excell3 became news headlines. He was suspended from the House of Lords for financial irregularities. Around the same time, he was forced to quit from his academy trust for other financial irregularities.

The offer arrived soon after. This time it was from a local authority just outside Birmingham and managed by a different council; this looked to be a good way forward.

## More Meetings

A meeting with the Director of Education for this new local authority followed. He was extremely impressed with the work of Excell3 and the various university partnership projects as well as the number of government policy groups they were part of.

'Cheron, it's clear you have the pedigree for a project like this; I will be delighted to put your name forward as the sponsor for our high school.'

Several meetings with the school followed. It's fair to say these meetings couldn't have gone any better. There was a real enthusiasm to work together expressed by the school's senior team.

Cheron had also been working hard to develop the appropriate external partners. Again, the University of Staffordshire agreed to offer support and a further relationship was developed with Wolverhampton Grammar School.

The main challenge as Stephen Brooks saw it was in taking over the school for the next academic year. This meant that the Excell3 team had to drop everything else and put together a major proposal in eight months rather than the usual two-year process. Due diligence, analysis, planning, reviewing the curriculum, identifying the local demographics – all had to be completed and presented to the council in a very short period of time.

Such an incredible effort went into developing the business plan, ensuring the financial support and completing the other formalities. All of this meant long hours as well as taking staff away from their work on other projects. But it would be worth it. After all, this was a long-term project, an exciting prospect and worth every moment of time and energy. And in spite of everything, everyone at the council and the school were on board, so what could possibly go wrong?

## Bolt from the Blue

The call from the Department for Education was a bolt from the blue.

'Doctor Byfield, we are sorry to have to advise you that the local authority has decided to pull out of the agreement – they no longer want you to sponsor their school.'

'Oh my goodness! Why?'

'Well, I think it best that you speak directly to their Director of Education. We are simply relaying the message we have received.'

Cheron was on the phone to the director straight away. What on earth had happened? It was hard to stay calm on the phone, hard not to shake with the emotion of it all. Could this possibly be happening all over again? It was hard to think straight, hard to pray. God, where are you in all of this? Why is this happening?

A couple of attempts to call the Director of Education eventually succeeded. An urgent meeting was arranged which Cheron and Henroy Green attended.

The Director of Education for the council went straight to the point.

'Cheron, Henroy, I'm very sorry we can't go forward with this sponsorship.'

'But why?' Cheron challenged. 'We are at a very advanced stage in our arrangements. I'm not aware that there are any problems with the school team. They seem very keen.'

'It's not the school itself, Cheron, it's a decision we made at the local council. It's been brought to our attention that you have links with a Pentecostal church. You share their offices and you have representatives from there on your board.'

'That's right. But why is that a problem?'

'Well, we knew you were Christians of course. But we didn't appreciate you were Pentecostal. Pentecostals are a cult. We cannot give one of our schools over to a cult so I regret we have to close down our discussions and plans. We are only going to be interested in secular sponsors.'

Cheron tried to keep the shaking out of her voice as she replied.

'Well, first of all, Excell3 is independent and we are an ecumenical Christian charity. But anyway, are you saying Pentecostalism is a cult?! That's simply not true! It is a mainstream denomination in this country. No way could it ever be considered a cult!' Pentecostals adopt the Nicene Creed as their statement of faith which is a defining creed for mainstream Christianity.

'Well that is the advice we have been given and we have accepted that advice. Regretfully, Cheron, we can't go ahead.'

'Oh goodness! This can't be happening. What you have been told is simply not correct. Please do your research – you will find that Pentecostal churches are part of mainstream denominations. They could never be considered a cult. I'll draw up a paper for you to show you.'

'Sorry, Cheron, it's too late. It's already gone to the council and the sponsorship offer has been withdrawn.'

'You mean you made the decision without consultation? Without checking with us?'

'Yes. I'm sorry. Even if you are correct, it's too late now, the councillors have already made the decision.'

## Boxing Ring

For Cheron, it felt like she'd been in a boxing ring as she headed back home. For this to happen again, and so soon after the College High experience, was almost too much to bear.

Clear injustice. Racial discrimination. Religious discrimination. Prejudice. Ignorance. All seemed to apply here. Cheron was sure she could cause a lot of trouble on this one if she wanted to. The rumours were that some councillors rather late in the day realised the Christian ethos involved with the proposal and were adamant they wanted a secular school.

All this was worthy of challenge. And yet, in her spirit there was just a suggestion that maybe God was in this.

**Peace**
**A King Solomon Value, the King Solomon Way**

The connection, the vine through which all blessings flow
Jesus Christ, He we may know

My Father in heaven as you sit above
Your countless showers of abundant love

In Christ alone my hope is found
Peace like a river, yonder bound

Your peace, still, radiant and calm
Jesus my Saviour, forever safe in your arms

Peace comes with the confidence you get deep down in your soul
From knowing that God is fully in control

So no matter what happens, the good or the bad
His peace will be the best friend you will have had

The peace of God is beyond our comprehension
It's a gift we get because of our God connection

**Sharmaine King – Primary Teacher, King Solomon International Business School**

It was hard to understand what had happened, but a peace from God began to rest on Cheron as she started to pray about what to do next.

Needless to say, the reaction from staff at Excell3 and other stakeholders was one of justified anger. They felt demoralised too. What was the use of working in this sector, helping young people make the best of their abilities when a local council could just decide to close a project down with no discussion or consultation?

The politics and pressure of trying to sponsor an academy was getting to Cheron and to her staff. Maybe it was best not to proceed? Maybe God had other plans? But there remained a niggle. Didn't God say to go for this? Just because there had been hold ups and disappointments, had God really changed His mind? Shouldn't they push on?

But how to do that?

The call from her friend Bethany was timely.

# Chapter Five – A Gift From The Father

Cheron and Bethany had first met at an educational event. Recognising each other's Christian faith, they would pray for each other's desire to serve God through their work. Bethany would regularly look for opportunities to help Cheron in her quest to sponsor a school.

Such an opportunity arose with the invitation to an event at the House of Commons. Chaired by Michael Gove, then Shadow Secretary of State for Schools, it was a gathering of representatives from Christian schools. Cheron didn't have a school, of course, but Bethany managed to get her an invite.

Cheron was given the opportunity to speak briefly at the event so she talked of the challenges she had been through in attempting to sponsor a school.

Following her talk, Michael Gove responded. Although not yet formally announced, he wanted Cheron to know of plans that the Conservative Party were drawing up should they come into power at the next election.

'Cheron, we are planning something completely new and exciting; we are planning to introduce free schools. These will be directly approved from Westminster and will allow faith and community groups like Excell3 to start up their own schools. The local authorities will not be able to interfere in the way they have with your attempts to sponsor.'

The idea for free schools was modelled on the USA charter schools. Charter schools are funded by the government but these schools are subject to fewer rules than traditional state schools. They are meant to assist underserved communities that wish to have alternatives to their neighbourhood school.

As she sat in her seat on the early evening train from Euston back to Birmingham, there was a smile on Cheron's face. Maybe this was the way forward? More of a challenge, of course, starting a school from scratch, but with less interference from local authorities and more of an ability to shape the school. It looked like a good way forward.

The new possibilities of a faith school would have to await the results of a general election. Only then would the team know whether there was a new opportunity and a new challenge.

In the meantime, Cheron faced a personal challenge of her own.

## We Will Carry You

'I'm sorry to have to tell you it's cancer.'

Called in to the consultant's offices a week later, Cheron was not expecting the news. She had had an exploratory biopsy and the results were in.

This was the second time. Cheron had first been diagnosed with cancer when she was young but it had been successfully treated. To have cancer again was devastating.

She tried to stay engaged with the consultant's words, but it was hard to concentrate. She felt numb. With no history in the family of any cancer and with a successful recovery this was not something she ever thought she would have to face again.

'What's wrong?'

Her sister Audrey was around at the house when Cheron got back, and she saw the look on her face.

'It's not good news.'

What happened next is a miracle. A miracle in a number of ways.

The first is the way friends and family gathered around. Audrey, along with friends Jacee, Gwen and Joy, formed different prayer teams. A number went on a partial fast for twenty-one days, including Audrey's teenage daughters Nicole and Crystal. Cheron herself was instructed not to fast but to keep up her strength.

'Cheron,' Jacee said one day, 'don't you fast. We will carry you.'

And they did. There were prayer nights, sometimes praying right through the night. There were further fasts. People called at the house to pray directly with Cheron. Her local church remained engaged in prayer. Other churches up and down the country were praying for her. People who had never met her had added her to their prayer list.

It was overwhelming. Cheron felt such love at a tremendously difficult time. She felt close to God, realising the love he had for her as a father. How she was under the shelter of his wing (Psalm 91) at such a difficult time.

## Healed

The twenty-one-day fast began exactly twenty-one days before the scheduled operation. At the start of that fast, Cheron met with Audrey, Jacee and Diane. Through the prayer time, they would break off to sing, declaring 'victory is mine', and calling on God for healing as they did so. It was a powerful time.

Cheron knew something had happened but wasn't sure what. She wanted her surgeon to do another test before conducting the surgery. She told the surgeon that she didn't think she needed the surgery anymore. But the response was, 'There isn't a hospital in this country that would not go ahead with this. It really is in your best interest, Cheron; it will be okay, don't worry.' They put Cheron's concerns down to pre-operative anxiety.

Just before Cheron went into theatre whilst praying with Audrey, Joy, who was leading one of the prayer teams, sent a text, quoting Jesus' words: 'With God all things are possible.' Cheron was peaceful and in faith that God would have the final say.

Following the surgery Audrey visited her in hospital on a daily basis. Audrey's faith in God was high. She had spent much time in prayer and fasting. On the first visit, she told Cheron that God had healed her. She played the song 'You deserve the glory and the honour' on her mobile phone. It was a song of praise to God, declaring that He deserves the glory because He does great miracles. It was a beautiful song, but Cheron didn't take Audrey's comments too seriously at first.

Cheron had been provided with a morphine pump to deal with pain relief.

But there was no pain at all.

The staff were amazed. The nurse commented that 'most patients would have used the morphine pump a hundred times by now!'

But not this time. Not once.

Another of the patients on the ward had observed Cheron and how she coped, noting too the number of visitors that had called to pray. She expressed amazement that Cheron was pain free.

'You've had a different kind of healing, haven't you?' she said.

Still waiting for the final say, Cheron reflected on the first time she'd had cancer. She remembered struggling to pray. And then one Sunday, whilst at church her eyes caught hold of a large scripture poster that had been on the wall for several years. Only this time, it spoke to her in a new way: 'I know the plans I have for your life.'

She was excited because if God had plans for her life that meant she would have a life. That meant she would recover from the cancer. A few weeks later, under the care of the anaesthetist whilst lying on the operating theatre table, out of the blue a very traditional hymn – not her favourite – flooded her mind, 'Be still, and know that I am God.' She later discovered that this was not just a song, but a scripture. It was actually the Word of God ministering to her (Psalm 46:10) just when she needed it, reminding her that He was in control.

Whilst Cheron was recovering from cancer the first time round, her best friend from childhood, Indrajit, became a Christian. Indrajit was from a Sikh background. She had always been very much anti-Christian, viewing the Christian missionaries historically as being racist imperialists – hence she wanted nothing to do with Christianity. But when Cheron became ill, Indrajit spent as much time as she could with her friend whom she had grown to care for and respect greatly. It was their close friendship that led Indrajit to accompany Cheron on a trip to Israel. Whilst in Israel, Indrajit did a deal with God. She prayed to God and said that if He spared Cheron's life, she would consider becoming a Christian. Consider? Not much of a deal. But whilst in Israel, she experienced the overwhelming love of Jesus. She set aside the deal and accepted Jesus as her Lord and Saviour. Indrajit returned to England as a Christian.

That first time Cheron did make a full recovery. God was in control.

As Cheron awaited the results the second time around, she reflected on that first healing and pondered whether she would need further treatment – chemotherapy, radiotherapy or both.

On the day Cheron was to be discharged from the hospital, Audrey came to collect her. It was as they were preparing to leave that the consultant arrived. The results of the operation were through. As he looked through the papers, the consultant looked puzzled. In silence he gazed again at the report, turning the pages, and then muttering the word 'bizarre' to himself. What was bizarre?

'Cheron, it's disappeared.'

'What do you mean it's disappeared?'

'There is no trace of the cancer at all. It's bizarre, absolutely bizarre. I've never known anything like it.'

Cheron and Audrey looked at each other. They said nothing, just stared at each other, but they were both thinking the same thing. 'Oh my God, it's happened!' A divine miracle.

Audrey turned to the consultant, hesitated, cleared her throat, and stutteringly asked, 'Are you sure?'

'Yes, I'm sure,' said the consultant. 'But I'll get this double checked anyway. It will take a couple of weeks. The hospital will get back to you.'

The result of the second test came back two weeks later and with it the confirmation the cancer had disappeared.

God had answered amazingly.

The prayers were answered.

No cancer. No chemotherapy. No radiotherapy. No treatment needed.

A miracle.

A gift from Father God for His daughter.

Much praise and thanksgiving was given to God.

Cheron later developed a website called Cheron's Story to share her testimony and give God the glory for what He had done. The instrumental background music she chose for her website was 'You deserve the glory and the honour'. God indeed deserved it all – all the glory and all the honour. He had performed a miracle.

Within weeks of the website being launched, Cheron was surprised to see how much interest it had attracted. Tens of thousands of people viewed it, including the Department for Education . . . The Department for Education? Why?

### A God of Miracles

As a hospital chaplain I appreciate the dedicated staff who invest so much in the restoration of people's health . . . I also have experienced the dramatic healing after prayer of those clinically diagnosed inoperable or terminal.

As faith is not in conflict with fact, the healings that I've been involved with have been endorsed by medical examination.

To see people moving out of palliative care, consultants visiting my office looking for answers, is humbling.

One minister's wife became nationally known through the media and by personal testimony after immediate remission from stage four cancer after prayer. She made the papers and the evening news in Northern Ireland.

Faith is more than mind over matter; it's spirit overriding intellectual preconceived ideas.

**Revd David Carr**

# The Fight To Start A Free School

# Chapter Six – Pushing Through, Staying True

Cheron's return to work coincided with David Cameron winning the UK general election in May 2010. With his appointment, the free schools programme had begun and Cheron was keen to put forward an application.

## Applications

The process was complicated and time consuming. Cheron tried not to disturb the day-to-day work for the majority of staff, with Dr Tony Talburt assisting her in developing the curriculum model.

By that time, the charity was involved in around twenty different projects throughout the UK and, hence, the daily workload was considerable. Nevertheless, this process was important to its community and the application went ahead.

One of the first essentials was to think of a name for the proposed school. Cheron held brainstorming sessions with Excell3 staff and board members. She wanted something that reflected both the Christian faith and the international business specialism of the school – the obvious passions of Cheron. In the Bible, King Solomon, a man with a strong belief in God, shown to be the wisest man that lived, was also a successful international business trader. And so the school was to be named King Solomon International Business School.

To ascertain whether there was a need for a faith school in Birmingham, Stephen Brooks gathered together a number of Bible school students from the nearby Andrew Wommack Ministries Charis Bible College. They carried out surveys on behalf of Excell3, gathering the necessary information and support.

In addition, numerous meetings were held with prospective parents at local churches and community centres in order to obtain the required support.

Eventually the bid was sent in and before long a reply was received advising that it had not been successful. The reply pointed out a couple of minor weaknesses. It would have been a matter of a few minutes' work to fix this but sadly, the way the Department for Education worked, it would be another year before a further application could be considered.

It was heart-breaking to have carried out all that work and not to have reached the interview stage. Nevertheless, Cheron pushed on and, in 2012, started preparing for a second application.

## What a Way Fe You Ches High

Cheron engaged the services of a company that supported free school applications. They were expensive but if it meant a successful application it would be worth it. However, at their first meeting, their condescending attitude reminded Cheron of the Patois dialect she heard when she was making enquiries about going to Oxford, 'What a way fe you ches high', which means a person is being far too ambitious.

The consultants clearly thought she was going above her station and tried to discourage Cheron from applying. As far as they were concerned, Excell3 didn't stand a chance as free schools were the domain of the 'big boys'. They went on to name a number of big companies and multi-academy trusts that were planning for free schools in Birmingham. They were indeed giants in comparison to Excell3. But for Cheron, God is bigger than any giant, so without the help of the consultants she pushed on with a second application.

This time there was a call to interview. The Department for Education had taken the bid seriously and it was with some fear and trepidation that Cheron and five of her team made their way down to London for the formal interview.

It was clear early on in the interview that they were not going to be successful. Cheron accepted that on one part of the bid, she had dropped the ball and not answered the questions sufficiently. The consequence, of course, was another year of waiting until a third application could be constructed and sent in.

In the meantime, with Excell3 having made a compelling case for a free school in Birmingham, the Department for Education accepted the need and approached one of their favourite academy trusts, asking them to set up such a school in the centre of Birmingham. No formal application was made; they were simply handed the school on a plate.

Cheron attended a large conference at the University of Birmingham. Up until then she hadn't been aware that some within the community knew of what had happened. That was until she heard the keynote speaker talk about the injustice of what had happened to King Solomon School. The case for a city-centre location had been stolen by others.

Injustice again. It was noted.

## The Strangest Feeling

Cheron still drove through a third application the following year. This time, she made sure that she had covered all her bases. She found another consultant. This consultancy was extremely helpful. They were enthusiastic about the bid and it again reached the interview stage. The consultant volunteered to join the panel for the interview at the Department for Education's offices.

Cheron and her team attended the interview with a degree of confidence. Along with the consultant, they were optimistic that they had a good application and had been thorough in their answers.

This changed the moment they went into the room.

Something was wrong. The interviewing panel appeared to be rather solemn. But it was more than that. The room had the strangest feeling.

There was an iciness to the whole process. It was as if the panel was just going through the motions, with no intention of approving the project.

The questions were answered well. The application stood up to scrutiny. But as they left that day, one of the team said that he had felt as if the whole meeting had been shrouded in hatred. This team member was a white local Birmingham business person, there to support certain aspects of the bid. He was shaken.

'Cheron, that meeting. There was hatred there! Hatred! The way they addressed you, the coldness of their answers. That was racism. Blatant racism!'

The consultant who attended the interview was baffled. He had been present at many interviews within the free school application process but claimed never to have experienced such coldness towards any of his organisations.

All the team had felt the iciness. Was it racism? Was it because of their Christian faith? Was there another reason? None of this would matter, of course, if the bid was accepted.

Weeks later, a formal letter was received. 'We regret to inform you . . .'

The consultant was in shock. All the other free school applications he had supported had been successful. As he saw it, the approval process should easily have been passed. Every aspect of the application had been thorough. All the questions were well answered. The vision was clear. The support was in place. The bid was compelling. It should have gone through.

The team at Excell3 were emotionally exhausted. They hoped Cheron had got the message that the Department did not want them and people of their background to be given a school.

'Cheron, can't you see? They simply don't want us! Whether it's the colour of our skin, our Christian faith, or some other reason, they are not going to approve us. Let it go. Let's get on with other projects where we are wanted!'

Cheron considered the comments carefully. She prayed about it.

There was to be a fourth application.

## The Surprise Meeting

News of the injustice spread throughout the community. Parents were angry. Local activists were calling for action.

Cheron was waiting for feedback on her fourth free school application. Then the email came. They had made it through to the interview round.

But another interview. She'd been here too many times now. She cried out in prayer to God.

'Lord, it's me again. Another interview. But with no political support, the Department will just be going through the motions again.'

Just as she finished praying, Cheron logged onto her computer and saw another one of those relatively frequent invitations to a meeting with a government minister. Baroness Warsi. Cheron was dismissive of it.

After a long day's work, Cheron headed for home. Just as she got into the car she received a call from Bethany, her trusted political associate. It had been a while. The last time they had spoken had been several years ago when they were both guest speakers at a national women's Christian conference. They had found a quiet room during the break time and prayed for each other, for Bethany's political career and for Cheron's desire to open a school.

They began to chat about their day and Cheron went on to talk about the invite from Baroness Warsi. Bethany was shocked with Cheron's dismissive attitude towards the invite.

'Cheron, an invite directly from Baroness Warsi! But she's a senior government minister, the Minister for Faith, and you're not going?'

'Bethany, I'm honoured to be invited, really I am, but I've got so much work to do. I'll make sure a member of my staff attends though.'

'No, Cheron, you've got to go!'

Bethany was very persuasive.

That evening Cheron sent off an email confirming her attendance.

The venue for the meeting was embargoed until the next day.

The confirmation came through. Cheron couldn't believe it. She assumed the meeting with the Baroness would be in London, but no, it was in Birmingham, and not just that, it was to be held just down the road from where Cheron worked. Two minutes' drive and she'd be there.

And that's when things got really puzzling.

As she drove up to the building, the area looked strangely quiet. Cheron knew this neighbourhood well. It's a district she had worked in for many years, close to where her office was located.

But today, it was quiet. Really quiet. Two police cars passed her on the road. The car park at the offices where the meeting was to be held was almost empty. It was always full, to the extent that Cheron had been wondering whether she would even get a space. But not today.

As she walked up to the main doors, things got stranger still. The person at the door was verging on inquisitorial as she asked Cheron why she was there. But there was such a change in tone as soon as Baroness Warsi's name was mentioned.

Once inside, Cheron could see Baroness Warsi talking to a few people. Cheron had never met the Baroness before, having only seen her on the television.

Cheron recognised the Baroness and walked towards her.

'Hello,' said Baroness Warsi, 'and who are you here to see?'

Cheron was a bit taken aback. It was a strange question for her to ask. The Baroness had invited Cheron to meet with her, so why was she asking her who has she come to see?

'Well . . . you actually.'

'No, you have not! No.' Baroness Warsi smiled. 'You've come to see David Cameron, the Prime Minister.'

There was no hiding the shock on Cheron's face! Meetings like this are often arranged under cover of something else to maintain the safety of the Prime Minister and to ensure the press are not present at times when they are not wanted.

Baroness Warsi briefed those attending regarding the protocols for meeting the Prime Minister and all then took their seats. The doors opened and David Cameron walked in with his entourage. Cheron had been invited to sit next to the Baroness and, to her surprise, the Prime Minister sat directly opposite Cheron. Face to face with the Prime Minister of the United Kingdom was not something Cheron had expected when she woke up that morning.

All the guests had business connections in the Birmingham area and each was asked simply to say what was on their mind. Other guests shared concerns regarding projects they were involved in. Then came Cheron's turn.

'Prime Minister, what's on my mind right now is my ongoing frustration in trying to start a faith school. We have been pushed back so many times now. We are doing all the right things, passing all the needed consent processes, but still, we are not getting through to final approval. In fact, so far no Christian school has been successful in getting approval in Birmingham.'

'That just shouldn't be the case. If your proposal is sound, you should get through,' said the Prime Minister. Turning to Baroness Warsi, he asked that the issue be taken up directly by her. He also asked Cheron to have a meeting with a senior government officer at the Department for Education. The only direct requests made that day by Prime Minister David Cameron.

Although Cheron did not hear directly from the Baroness, there was an obvious change in attitude at the next interview.

By now, the team had been pushed back three times. This was their fourth attempt. That's four sets of application papers. Four sets of public meetings in churches and communities in order to obtain the number of interested parents and pupils required. Four rounds of surveys, highlighting community support.

And with three previous refusals, it didn't get any easier. Why should the public continue to trust her? Why should any parent (yet again) say that their child would be a potential pupil at the school? No wonder the team had had enough. But Cheron was determined.

And with the meeting with David Cameron, even more so. Surely this was the opening she had needed to help obtain that elusive approval.

**Patience**
**A King Solomon Value, the King Solomon Way**

Patience, like a car to a stop sign, it waits in no rush,
Just like God waiting for His children to come to Him to receive His gentle touch

If you are pursuing something good, do not stop, says patience
Even if it's hard you can keep going, remember God's given you the licence

Face your challenges, don't take your flight
Face your challenges, come on, get up and fight

Patience will subdue frustration
In the face of an adverse situation

So be stubborn, determined and persistent
Resist rash reactions, be long tempered and resilient

**Oxford Class, King Solomon International Business School**

# Chapter Seven – Trying Again

There had been so many applications, so many disappointments, so many push-backs. But having got this far, there was no going back.

## Attempt Number Four

Excell3 decided to link up with an established education partner. A trusted friend scouted the country for a strong Christian education partner and suggested Woodard Schools, a large group of Church of England schools established since 1848. A meeting was arranged for Cheron to be introduced to Chris Wright, the Education Director for Woodard in a beautiful barn conversion in Hertfordshire. Chris Wright was impressed with the vision for King Solomon. He felt her vision was compelling. Excell3 was invited to become affiliated to Woodard and the offer was welcomed and accepted. This was the first time a non-Anglican school would be part of the Woodard family of Christian schools. Woodard has a growing commitment to support children from inner-city schools from deprived backgrounds and welcomed King Solomon into their family.

Each application round saw changes in the criteria. Each time it became more challenging. This time around, a principal needed to be in place ahead of the bid. But how could the team possibly achieve that? It was fine for established schools who could put forward one of their existing leaders; that was easy. But not for Excell3. To appoint to a position before the position existed seemed an impossibility. Nevertheless, the team advertised and made a good provisional appointment.

A lack of political support remained a problem for the team. Initially the leader for Birmingham Council had promised his backing, but when invited to write in support, he declined to do so.

Cheron decided to write to Michael Gove MP, by now Secretary of State for Education. It was a compelling letter but at the last minute Cheron felt a hesitancy in sending it, and it remained as a draft on the laptop.

## Mountains to Climb

Cheron went to church as usual. The prayer group she usually joined was not meeting before church that Sunday morning so she joined another group. She didn't know anyone in this group. But when they split up to pray in smaller groups, the group leader said:

'Cheron, God loves you. He really loves you.'

Then she said:

'You've got mountains to climb. I'm going to pray that God will level out those mountains.'

She prayed as though she had insight into each huge mountain Cheron had to climb before she could get the free school application approved.

## The Interview

On the day of the interview, a team of five travelled to London. This included the new principal designate as well as Chris Wright, the Director of Education for Woodard Schools.

It was evident that although Baroness Warsi had not been in direct contact, she had been working behind the scenes. The chair for the interview was none other than the director for the free schools programme.

There was one other face at the interview that Cheron recognised. An advisor to Michael Gove that had been on the interview panel the previous year. This was a surprise as the expectation was that the panel would always be replaced.

Having had the meeting with the Prime Minster, Cheron's colleagues wanted her to inform the panel of that meeting. Cheron refused to mention it. But she didn't have to as the first thing the chair of the panel said was that she was aware of Cheron's meeting with David Cameron.

## Adjourned

The interview went well. The questions were hard but fair and the atmosphere was so much better than the year before. The chair was supportive of the team and clearly impressed by the bid.

Then came the challenge.

The government advisor that had been on the panel the previous year, had been silent for much of the interview. As things came to a close, he interrupted. Let's call him Cain.

'There is just one concern I have. It relates to Doctor Byfield. Doctor Byfield, you have said on your website that God is greater than science.'

'Well, I am not aware of that being said on our site. Are you sure you have the right organisation?'

'No, not on the Excell3 website, on your personal website.'

'My personal website? I really can't remember saying anything like that. But that site is no longer online anyway, it hasn't been for many months.'

'Where's the evidence of her saying that?' said the chair.

'I don't have it on me now,' said Cain, 'but even if she has taken it down, I've cached it, so I can retrieve it for you, Madam Chair.'

The chair considered that in the light of this new evidence, the panel would need to look into it further and would therefore get back to Cheron within forty-eight hours. The meeting was adjourned. The team had to make their way back to Birmingham. They left the interview shocked and angry. They couldn't believe the interview had been adjourned because of a website telling of how God had healed Cheron. And for

Cain to raise this in such an aggressive manner right at the end of what had been to that point a successful interview, was quite simply wrong.

And now it made sense. That was more than probably the reason for the frosty interview the year before when the same government advisor had been on the panel. And now he was seeking, again, to influence the panel that following year. Was this the real reason for the previous refusal? And clearly, he was trying to do the same again.

As soon as Cheron got home from the adjourned interview, she checked her personal testimony from her earlier website. She couldn't understand the basis of his accusations. Nowhere had she said that God is greater than science. But what if she had? Her testimony on the site was all about giving glory to God, extolling His greatness and His ability to heal.

Who was Cain? The team did their due diligence. They found an article he had written in *The Guardian* newspaper criticising evangelical Christians, linking their schools with extremist Muslim and segregationist Jewish schools. The Evangelical Alliance had publicly hit back at Cain. They had strongly refuted his claims and criticised the government for demonstrating a 'woeful lack of religious understanding at the heart of government'.

It began to make sense. Understanding the bigger context was most helpful. Cain clearly had a personal agenda against King Solomon.

Two days later, Cheron received a call. It was Cain.

'Doctor Byfield, I am calling to say that upon further reading of your personal website, the panel has decided to continue with your free school application.'

There was almost an apology there. Not quite.

## Success

It was a Tuesday morning.

Cheron pulled into the office car park at just gone 8.30 in the morning. Some of her team were already in the office and there seemed to Cheron to be something of a hushed atmosphere as she walked in.

'Good morning, everyone.'

'Morning, Cheron!'

As she got to her desk, she saw it. Correspondence from the Department for Education.

A few seconds later, there was a shriek as she read the contents.

'We are pleased to confirm . . .'

It was done.

It was over.

The staff, well aware of what was on Cheron's desk, were crowding the door.

'Cheron . . . tell us. Please?!'

'We've got it! We've got the school!'

There were tears of joy in Cheron's eyes as she hugged each person there.

Four applications. Prejudice. Injustice. Lies.

All gone.

All gone in a moment of time.

Now to begin the real work.

**Joy**
**A King Solomon Value, the King Solomon Way**

Joy isn't necessarily about being happy,
It's the peace you get from trusting in God even when things are going badly

So even when life is not going so well
Joy continues to spring up like a living well

Joy is a moment of changing circumstances
It's not allowing situations to minimise our changes

Joy is a warm embrace from family, friends and loved ones
It's a contagious smile that lasts until the day is done

Joy is a friend who always finds the best in things
She is an underserved privilege worth more than diamonds and rings

Life is too short and unforgiveness is a waste
Of perfect peace and happiness reserved in your heart's special place

**Aaliyah Makaya – Year 10 Student, King Solomon International Business School**

## Excitement and Challenge

The team were excited. This was what they had been working towards for so long. Cheron made sure to take her senior team out for a celebration meal. There was a lot of noise, a lot of laughter and a lot of African and Caribbean food at the Akamba Restaurant. There was no doubt as to the sheer joy and elation on show at the restaurant that evening.

The local community were thrilled too. It had been so long. Many parents had faithfully supported each of the previous bids and, for them, the decision was a long time coming.

The government coordinated their approval letters with formal announcements in the press, so the next few weeks were full-on with interviews.

Along with the excitement of approval, there was an immediate problem. The principal designate decided not to take up the post just before the funding agreement from the government was due to be signed. She was not confident that the school would recruit enough children for it to be viable so remaining in her job was a risk she felt unable to take.

But it was a condition that the principal had to be in post before the funding agreement could be signed. The school was now at high risk of not opening. But the school had to open. King Solomon couldn't let parents down. For many, King Solomon was their first choice and, for some, their only choice as they had refused to select any other school. The school had to open.

The recruitment process for a principal commenced immediately. The Department for Education was involved. No suitable candidate was found.

A second round took place.

The panel wanted to appoint an experienced Christian principal but the establishment's representative refused to support the appointment. He was very keen on a Buddhist candidate. But this wouldn't be right for King Solomon.

A third recruitment round had to take place. Time was now running out. In the end compromises were made and Mrs Fatima was appointed as principal. Mrs Fatima did not hold a Christian faith.

It was only some years later that Cheron learned that the establishment's advisor did not have the authority to overrule the other three on the panel. But by then, of course, it was too late.

This was Mrs Fatima's first headship and was therefore a new challenge for her. She had a number of strengths. She was a very dynamic character and brought lots of enthusiasm to the post that was much needed in the school's formative year.

## Westminster

In the meantime, Baroness Warsi had actioned the request made by Prime Minister David Cameron, to organise a meeting between Cheron and the director for free schools to discuss the challenges the school had experienced in getting approval for their free school applications. The invite came. By now Cheron was becoming a regular visitor to Westminster, London.

Jeannette Veira, a board member for King Solomon, accompanied Cheron. They were surprised on entering the room to see a host of people around the meeting table, including the Department's legal advisor.

Cheron and Jeannette talked. The director listened.

'Madam, I hope you don't mind us commenting, but we need to challenge you about the lack of diversity amongst the decision-makers of free schools.

'Over the last three years King Solomon has attended several interviews and we have never seen even one black person involved on any of your panels. We know lots of interviews take place both here in London and in Sheffield, and most probably the problem is the same in Sheffield as well.'

Cheron and Jeanette went on to promote the need for the Department for Education free school decision-makers to be reflective of the community. It was clear the director was listening. She gave assurances to Cheron and Jeannette that the Department would address it.

A year later, Cheron and Carol, another board member, attended the schools pre-opening meeting with the Department at Westminster.

And this time a black woman was amongst those representing the Department for Education. Progress made.

Trial Again

And this time a black woman was amongst those representing the Department for Education, progress made.

# The Fight To Open A New School

# Chapter Eight – The Sign Of The Cross

The search was on.

With all things 'go' from the Department for Education, the emphasis moved to finding a premises. There was a lot to be done in a short time if the school were to open in September 2015. It was only in October 2014 that the approval had been given. But the team were used to tight deadlines.

The Education and Skills Funding Agency (ESFA) – the funding body of the Department for Education – were assisting with the search.

'Doctor Byfield, we have found three suitable properties for you to look at.'

## Property

The first looked promising but on closer inspection was too small. This left a choice of two. One was in the leafy suburbs of Edgbaston. A great building in good shape. The other was the old Waterlinks House building near to Aston University in the north of the city. Formerly offices, the complex had housed many companies such as British Gas and NHS offices.

Cheron and Stephen Brooks drove over to take a closer look at the Waterlinks House building.

'Sorry, Cheron, it's awful. I'm not even going to get out of the car to look at it. It's a waste of time. The whole place is a blot on the landscape! So dreary, so ugly! It's completely dilapidated!'

Stephen had made his feelings known. Ignoring the protests, Cheron got out of the car and looked around the outside of the building.

She too had no interest in Waterlinks House. Standing outside the building, she rang the authority and advised them to take Waterlinks House off the shortlist.

'Are you sure, Cheron? If I take it off and you don't find anything else, you won't be able to open the school in September, but it's entirely your decision.'

'Okay then. Let's leave it on for now.'

Cheron walked around the outside of the building again. On returning to the car, she was a little more optimistic than she had been initially.

'It's okay, Stephen. There's a lot to be done, but it might work for us. It's certainly big enough. I'm not ruling it out.'

Rolling his eyes, Stephen stared out of the window as Cheron started the car and drove to Excell3's offices.

Two days later they were back, this time being able to go inside the building. All Stephen can say about that second visit is that it was as if scales had been removed from his eyes. No longer did he see it as an ugly building and a health and safety hazard. Instead, he began to see what it might become.

'I've never known this to happen before, Cheron. I don't quite know what's happened. I can't ever remember changing my mind so quickly and so radically! I think this might work for us. I think we may have found our building!'

Back at the offices, one of Excell3's staff ran in to Cheron's office holding a map.

'Doctor Byfield, look! Look at this. Look at the name of the street Waterlinks House is on!'

And there it was. Lord Street.

The coincidences didn't end there. As they looked down at the map, they noticed for the first time, the outline of the actual building. It was in the shape of a cross.

Following further research, Stephen found that prior to Waterlinks House being built, there had been a school on the site, going back to the 1920s.

When does a coincidence become a God-incidence? The team was sure. The call to the establishment was made. The finances from the agency were released. The purchase documents were signed in April 2015. And the project began.

## Shot

The phone call came in on a Wednesday morning in May. An Ofsted rated outstanding school had agreed to be the education partner for the new school, helping and guiding them through the process. Their senior leadership team were to be involved: the principal, vice principal, head of teaching and learning, chief financial officer . . . King Solomon was set to be off to a good start.

But the call was to say they were pulling out.

Pulling out! The team was devastated. The school was pulling out because one of the teachers at their school had accidentally shot a student during a science experiment. He was sacked.

Thousands of students backed a campaign to give him his job back. The campaign was led by the student who was shot. He knew it was an accident.

It made headlines. The press were all over the story. The teacher was reinstated. The pressure on the school was immense. The headteacher left. The school was in a state of crisis. Whatever capacity they had before to support King Solomon during its pre-opening phase evaporated.

Cheron had to rescue this somehow and they were running out of time. They had no time at all to find another partner, so the only possible solution was for Excell3 to take the task on themselves and push through with the work that their partner school would have done on their behalf.

## To the Rescue

Another challenge the school faced was the urgent need for a base to operate from until the school property was ready for occupancy. Excell3 negotiated an excellent deal with the Church of God of Prophecy administrative offices for the school staff to be based there. The principal designate, Mrs Fatima, and all the newly appointed staff spent their early months at the church's offices. Meetings with the educational authorities took place there. Problem solved.

Cheron and Stephen already had their work cut out. Establish a bank account. Manage the project development grant. Manage the recruitment campaign. Draft the education brief. Manage the admissions process. Manage, manage, manage . . .

But even this was not going to be enough. Nowhere near enough.

Cheron was desperate. She needed a finance expert to take over in a finance director role. She called on Audrey, her sister, again. She was a qualified accountant with over twenty years' accountancy experience and had worked at director level within the higher education sector. Audrey had already played the leading role in preparing the five year budget for the free school bid and had attended all the Department for Education interviews. She knew them. They knew her. Now the free school proposal had been approved, as far as she was concerned, her role was over and she had passed the baton to the chief financial officer of the outstanding partner school.

But now the baton was back with her. Audrey volunteered her time and took over the finances for the pre-opening phase. Bespoke Terms of Reference. Sign-off from the Trust. Financial operating procedures. Pre-opening budget. Agreed parameters. The list of tasks went on and on.

The ESFA would not allow the school to tell the parents where the school building was going to be until the contract was signed. This left parents having to make major decisions about sending their children to

King Solomon without knowing the location. The most the team were permitted to say was that it would be near Birmingham city centre and not too far from Aston University.

## All Hands On Deck

Dr Tony Talburt, Excell3's education lead, had to be pulled off his work to develop the education brief and a high-level curriculum model. Esron Small, Excell3's in house graphic designer, supported the school with its marketing; the promotional brochures, leaflets, prospectuses, the banners and stands. He designed the logo for the school: a golden crown with a purple globe in the centre representing royalty, the international dimension of the school reflected in the globe, and at the centre of it all was the Christian symbol of the cross.

The regular pre-opening monitoring meetings which Cheron and Chris Wright attended with the Department for Education all went well. All milestones were met. But it was not just the pre-opening project plans that were subject to scrutiny but also Cheron and some members of the board. The establishment's questioning as to whether Clive Bailey was related to a Pastor Daisy Bailey in Manchester, seemed unnecessarily intrusive. He isn't, but what if he was? Another director came under scrutiny for one of the educational and cultural trips he had organised to Ghana. They wanted to know his relationship with two of the people who attended the trip. Nothing untoward had gone on. The level of scrutiny was over the top. Chris Wright, a white ally, disapproved of the way these black professionals were being treated. Directors felt like this was the equivalent to the stop-and-search racial profiling of black males. After the meeting Chris Wright advised Cheron not to be intimidated by them.

The team continued to work hard to complete the pre-opening action plan. They did this pro-bono.

This was all additional pressure they could have done without. Late nights. Early mornings.

But it was done.

The pre-opening plan was signed off by the Department for Education. Everything was in place.

# Chapter Nine – All Roads Lead To Lord Street

It's now 10am. A prayer team is waiting at the Lord Street entrance for the landlord to open the gates. But where is he? Why hasn't he opened up? Had we been gazumped? Has another group made a better offer? Cheron's head was spinning with questions.

'Okay,' says Bishop Wilton Powell, 'we may not be able to go inside the building, but nothing can stop us from praying outside at the gates.'

It's winter, it's cold, very cold, but Cheron, Clive and the guests stood outside the gates and prayed. Bishop Alfred Reid prayed for the situation with the landlord and for blessing on all those who would enter through the gates.

Then Audrey prays. Whilst praying she sees an image of a whole host of people waiting at the gates to enter the school. Students. Parents. Staff. Churches. Volunteers. Businesses.

When Audrey finishes praying, she turns to Cheron and says:

'Cheron, it's not just us that want this school. There's a host of people waiting for this too!'

It's a humbling thought.

## The Lord Street Bus

On her way home, Cheron begins thinking about the host of people waiting to come to the school. She thinks ahead. She dreams of the opening day with the staff they had already appointed and the students they had already recruited. She envisages the students, on that first day the school would open. All of them travelling on an imaginary bus towards Lord Street.

The imaginary bus full of a motley crew of students reaches its destination – Lord Street.

Mrs Bim Oyede, the head of primary, lets the little four-year-olds off the bus first. Some are crying, some giggling, others pushing and shoving each other. Many have never let go of their mothers' apron strings before, so going to school is a traumatic experience for them.

Sue, Lin, Pete and Prinam, mainly primary school staff, help the little ones off the bus, gently reassuring those who are crying.

Sue Barton takes the names of all the Breakfast Club children. She'll do a good job of making sure they are fed and ready to learn.

Mr Hinds, the head of secondary, stands at the front of the bus. With a stern face he raises his right hand high, waiting for the Year 7s to be quiet. They dare not mess with Mr Hinds. He is something of an authoritarian teacher who has recently arrived from Jamaica. He is strict, real strict. There's deadly silence.

'Okay,' says Mr Hinds, 'you may go now. But walk off the bus in an orderly manner, no running.'

As they leave the bus, Dawn, Lorraine, Alisha and Jemini, mainly secondary school staff, direct the Year 7s into the school. Keeping them in order is a challenge though.

Students come from all sides of the city of Birmingham and as far away as Coventry and Sandwell. Some even from Manchester, with families there having heard the news of the Christian faith school.

A high percentage are from the wards of Aston, Lozells and Handsworth, where unemployment is three times the national average, with high levels of deprivation and high crime rates, especially with gun and gang crime.

Students are from a wide range of socio-economic backgrounds too. So off the bus come pastors' children. Lawyers' children. Doctors' children. Gangsters' children. The poor. The rich. Refugees. Asylum seekers. Children of the unemployed.

Stepping off the bus are churched children holding their Bibles. Some from the traditional churches: Church of England, Methodists, Baptists. The Pentecostals and charismatics are also equipped with tambourines, guitars and drum sticks ready for a lively assembly. Still others hold the Koran, the Vedas, Wicca, and the Guru Granth Sahib.

The Lascars, students from abroad, who have always felt abandoned and rejected in this country, are hopeful that this school will accept them.

A Christian school? The atheists weren't sure they were on the right bus!

Some of the boys have their fists clenched together ready to fire the first blow. The look on some of their faces is as if to say, 'Don't look at me too hard, otherwise I'll knock you down.'

Some unruly children have their passports in their bags – their mothers were going to send them away to be schooled in the Caribbean, but then they heard about King Solomon; there was hope!

Postcode rivalry between the Johnson Crew and Burger Bar gangs raises its ugly head. Some have beef with each other and scores to settle. In the middle of them are Catholic children making the sign of the cross as they leave the bus.

Onlookers are shocked. This is not what they were expecting. Were they expecting a bus full of angelic children with large glowing halos? Really?!

Bishop Powell and Bishop Reid stand outside the school gates whispering a prayer as the motley crew walk through the school gates and into day-one.

## School Guardians

This motley crew of students and all those yet to come throughout the years, needed to have guardians with a strong Christian faith, heaps of commitment along with stamina and resilience to act as guardians to this extremely challenging and complex new all-through school with its Early Years, Primary, Secondary and Sixth Form. This was complex.

Amongst the guardians ready for battle to defend and protect the King Solomon School vision were Trust members David Illingworth and Jeannette Veira. They were accompanied by directors Carol Brown, Clive Bailey, Dr Mark Yeadon, Dr Tony Talburt and Revd Brown.

But the motley crew were also going to need spiritual guardians on an operational level, providing spiritual support. Michelle Grannell, Pastor Doreen Makaya and Martyn Blunt were to play key roles. They were joined by the Order of St Leonard.

## Order of St Leonard

The Order of St Leonard is the faith authority for King Solomon.

'Cheron, you do know the Order of St Leonard will expect the school to commit to global Christian unity? There will always be things upon which Christians disagree; scriptural interpretation, doctrinal structure; the how's and whys of how we worship, pray, celebrate and reach out to the unsaved. But the fundamentals have to be there.'

'Yes,' said Cheron, 'we know that.'

'You see,' continued Revd Carr, 'what connects Christians is far greater and more powerful. Collective faith, good works, vision for the lost, our resources and capacity.'

'Yes, I know.'

'We believe that Christians should stay within their own church, their own community, their own denomination, because this brings the richness and diversity that is so vital in reaching the lost on both a global and a local level.'

'Totally agree, Revd Carr.'

'We expect the school to actively get involved in global social action, seeking to meet the needs of the poor, the needy and those less fortunate than us.'

'We are on the same page, Revd Carr. And by the way, we are using the Fruit of the Spirit as our character development framework. Are you okay with that?'

'Okay with that? Most certainly! That's music to my ears.'

## Gripped by the Vision

Cheron had met Michelle Grannell several months before during a visit to an Anglian church, when Cheron gave a presentation about King Solomon School.

Michelle was part of the ministerial team at the church. She stood out for Cheron as she was multi-tasking, ministering and mothering at the same time.

Dressed in her formal ministerial attire, Michelle was keeping an eagle eye on her own little children who would have preferred to be running around the church building rather than sitting quietly in the pew as Mum wanted. At times Michelle gave them that strict motherly look – the 'you dare do that again' stare. At another time she pointed her finger at them then quickly composed herself when she remembered that she was in full view of the congregation.

Now several months later a woman is sat in front of Cheron being interviewed for a senior leadership job at the school. At first Cheron didn't recognise Michelle, then it all came flooding back. Michelle interviewed very well indeed and was by far the best candidate. She had an amazing grasp of the vision. Shortly afterwards she was being welcomed on board the team at King Solomon.

Although small in stature, Michelle is one of the visionary giants at King Solomon. King Solomon is a life vocation that the Lord has led her to.

Michelle had been in a good job and was happy there. But then she saw an advertisement on Facebook for a job at King Solomon. She wasn't looking for a job but felt compelled to apply. Her headteacher tried to dissuade her from leaving: 'You can't work for a free school, you need your head testing. And it's less money than you are on.'

Her headteacher offered her promotion.

But this job wasn't about money. Michelle was caught by the compelling vision Cheron had shared when she gave the presentation at her church.

Michelle took the pay cut and came to King Solomon. She goes the extra mile because she knows she is not working for a school; she is working for God.

Still multi-tasking, at the school, she keeps one eye on teaching the children and the other eye on the direction of the school. Advising staff, she'd say, 'Stick to the vision, that way you can't go wrong.' She noted that the teachers who struggled with the Christian ethos, the international business emphasis and the stress on character development didn't tend to last long.

## Turbulence Ahead

Just before King Solomon was due to open, Audrey attended a conference in France. Pastor Doreen was there as well. Returning from the conference, the two sat next to each other on the plane. With nothing better to do, Audrey began to talk about this new school called King Solomon that was to open in Birmingham and the challenges the school had faced which God had enabled them to overcome. Audrey needed to talk and Pastor Doreen wanted to listen. But the flight wasn't going too well. There was some turbulence. The plane was being tossed to and fro. Then the turbulence became severe; then very severe. But Audrey was oblivious to it. She just kept talking about the school's vision, the challenges it had overcome, the excitement of opening. Pastor Doreen kept listening – whilst earnestly, but quietly, praying that they would survive!

They did.

Several months later Pastor Doreen was searching online for a placement to complete her chaplaincy course. She had no idea King Solomon even had a chaplaincy service. As soon as she saw King Solomon, she knew God was directing her to the school.

She made a tentative enquiry via Audrey. Immediately the doors were flung open. She became fearful and shut the idea down. She knew there were going to be challenges, but also the experience of a lifetime. She prayed, braced herself and went forward again.

Pastor Doreen attended the school for a preliminary chat with Mrs Fatima, the principal, and Mrs Bim Oyede, the head of primary. Bim's excitement about the school was infectious. She made Pastor Doreen feel so welcome.

Pastor Doreen had taught business studies in schools and colleges for over thirty years and had been a senior pastor for many years, but this was different. She was now in a Christian business school. She couldn't believe all that Bim was saying. If it was true, it would be the first school she'd ever been to where she could freely mention the name of Jesus, could offer prayer, could encourage both spiritually and academically and combine the two. It felt too good to be true. Everything Pastor Doreen heard made her heart leap.

It only took that preliminary chat. Once all the checks were completed, she was handed the school timetable, keys and a fob – all on the same day as the chat! Well, she knew now that there was no turning back.

As Pastor Doreen left the school that day, it was with a mix of excitement and concern – an awareness as to the cost of the steps she was taking and an excitement for the journey ahead. She was pleased to be there, but she knew too that there would be turbulence ahead!

## It's Too Big

Martyn Blunt is a Methodist. He volunteers his services, helping with student recruitment and more recently as a chaplain.

Martyn was introduced to Excell3 in 2014 whilst a headteacher at another school.

Before a new school opens it has no children of its own, yet promotional materials must be produced to help with recruitment. Martyn solicited parental consent from the school he was working at to allow their children to be photographed in King Solomon's school uniform for their promotional material.

But it was more than helping with photographs. Martyn was an inspiration to Cheron. When she had visited the school he was heading up, she was impressed by the way he had developed a strong Christian ethos. Little did Cheron know that Martyn was to become the head of the primary school and then later to join the chaplaincy team. Consequently, much of what Martyn was doing at his school would be carried over to King Solomon with his appointment. And from Martyn's point of view, his new appointment was an answer to a word God had spoken to him twenty-seven years before.

It was in 1990, when Martyn had been working for Scripture Union. His work had taken him to the prayer meeting held at the offices of Youth for Christ in Sutton Coldfield. The team there took time to pray for Martyn that morning. He felt a powerful sense of God's Spirit on him; so much so, he slipped from his chair onto the floor with a feeling of being pressed down.

As he lay on the floor, with the team still praying for him, God gave him a vision. Martyn is the first to admit that he doesn't often get visions or prophetic words, so this was special. In the vision, he saw a large building on the horizon and, as he looked, the building grew larger and larger, dwarfing the buildings around it.

The vision was so vivid that Martyn began to shout out, 'Lord, it's too big, it's too big!' He was overwhelmed with what he was seeing.

He agreed with his friends who were praying for him, that he would see that building somehow, in the future. But as the years went by, with no sign of any such building, the memory began to fade.

Martyn had almost forgotten about it. But God had not.

**The Motley Crew . . . We Are All on the Same Journey**

We are all on the same journey.
Our vision to achieve educational excellence, develop our character, be equipped to live, work and trade in the global economy and to be successful.

We are all on the same journey.
A journey of lifelong learning where we pursue learning in every environment possible. School. College. University. Home. Church. Work. Business. Leisure. Locally. Nationally. Internationally.

We are all on the same journey.
A journey developing our character. We not only have concern for others but we take action to show we care. We commit to a lifestyle of social action initiatives, we treat people rightly even when they don't treat us well.

We are all on the same journey.

We are positive. Peacemakers. Polite. Resilient in the face of challenge. We do the right thing, even when it's unpopular. Reliable. Trustworthy. We exercise self-control.

We are all on the same journey.

So please be patient with us if we've not quite reached there yet. We will get there because we have all been impacted by the vision of King Solomon International Business School.

**Grace Taylor – Volunteer, King Solomon International Business School**

# Chapter Ten – Building Dedication

Cheron's vision of that opening day with the motley crew was still a future event. In the meantime, there were tasks, challenges and some very long working days.

Some parents decided to do their own search to locate the school. They drove around the city centre and its neighbouring areas, trying to guess which building it was likely to be. But no one guessed it was the landmark building Waterlinks House!

Despite not knowing where the school building was, parents had a strong interest in sending their children to King Solomon. The vision was compelling. They applied. The school was oversubscribed. Cheron applied to the Department for Education to increase the size of the school. Approval was granted. Even after the school's successful expansion plans had been approved the school was *still* oversubscribed. It was one of the few free schools in the country to be oversubscribed before opening.

## No Problem

'No problem, ma'am, we will have at least some of the premises ready for September. Certainly, enough for you to move in.'

Cheron looked up at the seven-storey office complex with a raised eyebrow. But in the end, she believed what the builder was telling her. Why shouldn't she? He was the expert after all.

It turned out he wasn't so much an expert as an optimist.

The plan was to complete the ground floor and first floor – enough to start the school – and the rest could happen later.

At the various parents' evenings running up to the opening, Excell3 staff would welcome potential parents and pupils on the ground floor, where the reception area looked in good condition, and then escort them into the lifts, taking them to the fifth floor. Here, too, there was a small area that gave the impression of being quite reasonable and this was where the presentations were made.

## The Event

Mrs Fatima was busily preparing for the school opening. A small number of staff had been employed before the open date. Mrs Fatima was particularly impressed with Stephen Brooks. With his commitment and his work ethic, he was just the type of person she wanted working with her at the school. She employed him.

But the handful of staff were not enough to get the rooms ready for the opening. The lorry had dumped all the new furniture in the car park. Mrs Fatima reached out for help.

Audrey galvanised the support of her husband's nephews. These were strong young men. But the school had no budget to pay them. A bucket of KFC. That was the deal. It was enough. But when they arrived, they were shocked. The sheer volume and bulkiness of the furniture! However, a deal is a deal. A bucket of KFC it was.

Mrs Webley, one of the teachers, also called on the support of some of the young people from her Seventh Day Adventist Church, and together they got it done.

The building was now ready for the dedication service. The school's faith authority, the Order of St Leonard, led the service. About 100 people from a range of denominations attended.

Ian Burnelle, a member of the building contractors' team who lived in Bristol, was a Christian. He brought his worship team up with him to lead the worship.

It was a powerful moment in the journey. As Bishop Wilton Powell prayed a dedication prayer, there were tears in the eyes of many. What a journey. What a moment. Despite the setbacks, God had been faithful. In front of the, albeit unfinished, massive landmark building, a declaration was made to the city of Birmingham that God answered prayer, that He was a Father with a heart for His children, that generations to come were to benefit from the pioneering spirit He had promoted. Every room in the building was prayed for. Every student, parent and staff member were prayed for.

Ian's worship team led powerfully declaring the kingdom of God in the school.

## Thanksgiving and Prophetic Prayer

Father God, this is the beginning of this school. They will face opposition along the way. There will be those who will give a negative interpretation, those who will look for defects, those who will look for faults and those who will always be the first to say, 'This is not right.' But I pray that there will be grace in the school, a sense of sufficiency and mercy and goodness. I pray that there will be vision, inspiration to lift this school.

The three Hebrew boys in the Bible who went to Babylon made a commitment that they would not sacrifice their moral or ethical principles for the high and lofty god. We are praying that in this school there will be a mark, a distinction, there will be a statement made by the achievements, the sense of humanity, love, and that of outreach.

Birmingham is a city of industry, a city in the very heart of the nation and, Lord, let the heart of the nation prosper because men and women from this school will speak and act in such a way for the development of mankind and the development of the world.

There is disparity between nations, there is inequality, there's injustices across the boundaries and we need leaders who will be able to stand in the gap, to make up the edge and to make the difference. Here is a school who are preparing men and women to stand in this age with effectiveness, spirituality, moral and ethical principles, to speak that which you will have them to say. Men and women who are fearless and bold, whose character will stand as a beacon on the horizon, who will communicate in their languages and speak as you give them authority. We thank you, Lord.

**Prayer by Bishop Wilton Powell OBE, 2015**

Now the builders needed to deliver on their promise.

It didn't happen.

## Portacabins

The main contact with the builders was via the funding agency, the ESFA. For a while the builders kept them at bay, assuring them that all would be well. It was only when Stephen Brooks began to ask questions on the school's behalf that it came to light that this was the first such project this company had undertaken. A Scandinavian owned business, they had sent in a competitive bid, possibly to get a foot in the door of the lucrative education market in the UK.

Now they wanted to negate certain aspects of the contract. Instead of putting a brand-new roof on the building, they wanted to patch it up and give the school just a one-year guarantee. Instead of building a brick constructed sports hall they wanted to give the school a fabric framed sports hall. This could simply not contain any form of heat and would only be 10 degrees Centigrade warmer than whatever the temperature was outside.

Cheron could picture the children shivering with cold in the autumn and winter months. She was not prepared to accept this. Cheron insisted that a suitable sports hall was built. And a sports hall that could be used for assemblies – an important component for any faith school. She complained to the authorities. They listened.

In the end, the Education and Skills Funding Agency dismissed the builders. All building works ceased. But not just for a week or two . . . for months on end. Another building contractor had to be procured. This took time. But parents didn't want time. They weren't interested in the procurement process. All they knew was that for months, every time they walked past the building, nothing was happening. There was not one single builder on site.

Builders were at long last appointed. The new builders insisted on starting again. They had their own standards and their own materials, so even the new fittings already in place from the first company were taken out.

This was all well and good, but the money spent so far was still recorded as used on the project, thus reducing the budget for the school. And time was the other factor. Now the whole process was well behind schedule. The removal of the original contractors, the delay in tendering for new partners, the redesign . . . it all meant that September completion was looking to be a long shot.

But what to do? Stephen had noticed that on the building plans, a car park was included. He had initially been afraid to ask about this in case his questions resulted in the car park being sold off. It had not been discussed in negotiations and Stephen wondered whether it was in the plan as an oversight. Prayers were answered – the car park was part of the Waterlinks site, despite being situated across the road.

Not only did this give more acreage, but it also suggested a possible solution to the need to open in September. What if some temporary classrooms were placed on the car park? This would give the builders the extra time they needed and ensure the school could still open.

The establishment agreed to the plan and two large grey portacabins were erected in the car park.

The builders agreed that the students could temporarily move into the first two floors of the building upon opening in September to give the look and feel of a finished project. Then the students would be moved out to the portacabins for a few months to ensure completion.

A few months. If you talk to Stephen about it today, you get a wry smile. The builders took two and a half years in total to complete the five floors required for the school.

Two and a half years in portacabins. Two and a half years of noise, with no soundproofing. Then two and a half further years with inadequate buildings. Two and a half years of being hot in summer, freezing in winter.

## Joy

All this was to come though. In those heady days of early summer 2015, even with the possible alternative of portacabins, all looked well. Staff recruitment was going well too. A number of staff felt called to work at King Solomon. It's not every day a Christian faith school opens in inner Birmingham, in fact it was the first to cater for secondary age students and it attracted several mature teachers ready to forgo their current salaries for a lower income and the opportunity to pioneer something new.

Not all Christians either. One of the new recruits was Jemini, a Hindu. For Jemini, the attraction as a secondary school teacher was the faith ethos. The plan was to develop the school ethos around the theme of the Fruits of the Spirit in the Bible – love, joy, peace, patience, kindness, goodness, trustworthiness, gentleness and self-control. The idea that students would not just be challenged academically, but at a spiritual and personal level too was an attraction for Jemini.

Jemini even loved the planned prayer times within the school day. Students of all faiths and none attended these, so it would not be unusual to see a Muslim girl pray out, following on from a Christian boy once he had finished praying. Jemini finds these times are character developing, with the faith emphasis ensuring that students have an increased respect for the school and its values, all of it supported by a focus on the Fruit of the Spirit.

One of those virtues of the Fruit is joy, and that was the predominant feeling as the day for opening finally arrived. Teachers had to work hard for that day to come to pass though, using their own time and some choosing to use their own resources to make it happen.

Those early days were full of challenges, but also with such an awareness of oneness. The teachers were together on a mission. There was a strength and a camaraderie that many staff had not experienced before that time, and it remains a strength in the school to this day.

With last-minute additions to the décor of the classroom, at the personal expense of some of the teachers, like Michelle – it was a thrill for Michelle to hear the comments from parents as they toured the portacabins on opening day.

It is worth noting that staff such as Jemini and Michelle were very much the norm in terms of commitment as the school opened. All staff had to work a tremendous number of hours, well beyond that prescribed, to ensure the school opened on time and with some semblance of order. Specialist roles were a thing for the future. For now, the staff had to fulfil two or more different jobs. A teacher may well have ended up teaching two or even three subjects.

It takes exceptional staff to birth a school.

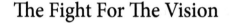

The Fight For The Vision

# Chapter Eleven – Open Gates

What a day – 2nd September 2015. The day the dream became a reality. All those years of applications. All those push-backs. All that prejudice. All of it overcome with the unlocking of the gates on that September morning.

*This is the day that the Lord has made, I will rejoice and be glad in it.* This is the scripture that echoed in Cheron's ears as she walked through the gates. As those gates opened, it was a declaration of God's answers. Not only open gates, but an open heaven.

## Unlocking

There had been so many participating in this journey. So many involved in unlocking the padlocks, pulling back the bolts, pushing the gates.

Cheron recalled Lin Taylor, the PA to the principal, who saw a beacon of light radiating from the building and out into the community.

Then there was Brigitta, a barrister who visited the school before the building was purchased, concerned about how the children were going to get to the school. She prayed about it and, whilst praying, had a vision of the school building. The building looked completely pure, and there were angels on top of the roof. She was reassured that all would be well, that children would want to come. And when the school opened it was over-subscribed. Later, Michelle Grannell was able to capture a photo of a rainbow over the building symbolising God's promises, mercy and faithfulness.

Dr Mark Yeadon, before he knew that the empty Waterlinks House had been bought by the school, felt compelled to pray for the building. His desire was that the building be used as a Bible school. And in a way it was.

It was hard for Cheron not to shout out her praises and thanksgiving to God as she remembered the visions of so many people, fulfilled that day as the gates opened. King Solomon International Business School. Just the name of it was enough to fill her with joy! Here it was. Right in the centre of Birmingham. In a challenging area of the city. And with the gates flung open to a new day and a new challenge.

Martyn had tears of joy in his eyes too.

Martyn's vision of the building that God had shown him all those years ago was now being fulfilled in front of him. Just a few days previously, as he had driven over the Aston Expressway, he'd seen the Waterlinks building to his left. It was at that moment he realised that this was the picture God had given him. This was the thing that was 'too big'. This was the building he had seen on the horizon in that vision years earlier, with the building getting taller and taller. Such an enormous building. Such a landmark. And here he was, a part of that 'too big' story, a part of the very thing God had spoken of.

What a sight! What a moment!

A faith school in the middle of Birmingham, at the sign of the cross.

The dream had become a reality.

## Matriculation

During her studies at Oxford, Cheron had been particularly impressed with the way the university formally welcomed new students into the university. Matriculation is the name they gave it. This was marked by its new students walking down the streets of Oxford dressed in their full gowns and caps. The Oxford University identity cannot be unwoven from its Christian past. Its buildings bear Christian names, its colleges all maintain a separate Anglican chaplaincy, its various charters bear seals of the head of the Church of England.

Why not do something similar for King Solomon students? Were the students there any less important than those at Oxford? Was their welcome not also worth celebrating?

And so, the annual matriculation ceremony was born.

Matriculation? What's that? The staff asked. The parents asked. The children asked. And the little ones struggled to pronounce it – but had a good try! Cheron had to explain time and time again, that it was a formal way of welcoming the students to King Solomon.

It had to be done correctly. Gowns were needed. Stephen pulled in favours from one of the women at his church to make 96 gowns for the eleven-year-old children, and 60 sashes for the four-year-olds.

But where could it be held? The school building was still under construction. It had to be off site. A beautiful hall at the Botanical Gardens was booked, and a coach hired to transport the children to the event.

Everyone wanted it. But no one quite knew what to expect. The air was filled with excitement and anticipation.

As the parents and invited guests sat quietly in expectancy of the event, soft worship music filled the air. Then the much-awaited announcement was made that the children were ready.

Mrs Bim Oyede marched in with the little four-year-old children following behind. Some were excited, some were crying. They all looked amazing in their purple school uniforms and gold sashes draped over their shoulders.

Mr Hinds, that strict head of secondary, made sure his motley crew of Year 7s were under control before they entered. In his usual Mr Hinds style, he raised his right hand and waited for the Year 7s to be quiet.

'Okay, Year 7, stand up straight, hold your heads high and follow me.'

The secondary students, dressed in gowns of bright purple, marched in to a Whitney Houston song, 'The Greatest Love'. The song reminded everyone that children are indeed our future.

It was an emotional time. An historical event, never forgotten.

Dignitaries attended and the press reported on it.

These children had a vision. They knew why they were at this school. Cheron asked the Early Years students and then the Year 7s what that vision was. They recited the school vision confidently and in unison:

*My vision is to achieve educational excellence, develop my character,*
*be equipped to live, work and trade in the global economy and to*
*be successful.*

In addition to the vision statement, a positive and reaffirming school declaration was written by Pastor Doreen. This is not just recited on a one-off basis, but posters have been developed and mounted throughout the school as a constant reminder.

**Students' Declaration**

I am a student at King Solomon International Business School, a school where God's presence is recognised and where the Bible is central.
I have wisdom far beyond my years.
I am an extraordinary person with incredible abilities which I will use to add value to others lives because I know that in helping others reach their dreams, I will automatically reach mine.
I am a good person. I love knowledge. I am always ready to learn.
(Based on Proverbs 18:15)

**Best**
I will do my best and my best will be good enough because the Lord will help me. (Based on Joshua 1:9 and Isaiah 41:10)

**Purpose**
God has a special purpose for me and I will distinguish myself in my field. (Based on Psalm 138:8 and Jeremiah 29:11 )

**Exceed**
I will exceed the expectations of those who have low expectations of me because I am the head and not the tail. (Based on Deuteronomy 28:13)

**Excel**
Where I have failed, I will succeed, and where I have succeeded I will excel. I am reaching forward in Jesus' name. (Based on Philippians 3:13)

There was such a buzz. Each student whose parents had given consent, walked through a tunnel of prayer formed by the Order of St Leonard and local clergy. They were all prayed for and presented with a Gideon's Bible. Then there was the celebration. Genuine worship and thanksgiving to God for all He had done, for the school, the staff, the students; for all the achievements so far.

An old hymn rang out at the end of the celebration followed by the Terry MacAlmon song 'You Deserve the Glory'. This was the same song that Audrey had played to Cheron before she'd had confirmation of her miraculous healing from cancer. The same one that Cheron played as background music on her website. There were tears on parents' faces.

Many parents, children and guests raised their hands in worship. The matriculation ceremony exceeded everyone's expectation. It was a glorious affair.

Everyone, Christians and non-Christians alike, staff, parents and the community, were acutely aware that King Solomon was history in the making, that it would be an adventure, that it was going to be tough, but that the love of God was going to be key to sustaining them. This razor-sharp awareness was reflected in a Thought for the Day, which Mrs Fatima read out:

'Today is important as it marks the opening of a new book, with many chapters to come. Books can be about adventure, and I think of the adventure that we are embarking upon as a school community. This book is also a love story. A love story between us and God, between staff and our students, with our loving community and parents, carers and supporters. Like any love story, true love is unconditional, it is unrelenting in the face of adversity and holds good when the tide rides high. It does not falter when times get tough, it does not forget in times of success. It persists and encompasses everything we do, just like the love for our school. Our part in the story is to climb Mount Everest. It will be hard work; it will take faith and dedication. When you reach the top of the mountain you will look down at the beautiful view and you will understand why God led you to us and why you are part of the King Solomon family.'

At the end of the ceremony, Cheron led the children marching out holding the Union Jack and King Solomon International Business School flags. The children marched out in an orderly fashion. Mr Hinds made sure of that. Accompanying the march was a school song which the Asian Christian Fellowship had helped the school to write:

*Education excellence*

*King Solomon, King Solomon*

*Character development*

*King Solomon, King Solomon*

As parents and guests headed towards the gardens, they were very vocal in their feedback.

'It's absolutely fantastic that King Solomon has become a reality.'

'My eyes were filled with tears as I saw the children marching in.'

'Today has been history in the making.'

'It's been just brilliant; it's out of this world.'

'It's exceeded my expectations.'

Matriculation was to become one of the important events in the King Solomon calendar. Cheron recalls one matriculation ceremony held at offices of Birmingham City Council. Lots of photographs were taken in the city centre. The children were the centre of attention as passers-by watched them assembled in the street for their photo shoot. All dressed in purple gowns and holding the Bibles they had just been presented with. Cheron recalls the photographer instructing the children to put down their Bibles for a photo shoot, and hearing a student say, 'Why do we have to hide our Bibles?' So many of these children were proud to be in a Christian school. Already those that had taken up the option of receiving a Bible were valuing what they had been given.

A time to remember when you're in the valley. There had been a few valleys already. And more to come.

The words of Psalm 23 sounded in Cheron's mind as she watched on. *Even though I walk through the valley . . . You are with me.* He was. And He would be.

## Number 10 Downing Street

Early on from the opening of the school, Cheron received an unusual invitation. Number 10 Downing Street. Prime Minister David Cameron was hosting a special event in celebration of free schools at Number 10.

Cheron arrived in plenty of time for the security checks.

Behind the iconic brick façade and the infamous black door are many elegant rooms, the home and office of British Prime Ministers.

The building is famous for its outside entrance: a single white stone step and black steel door with the number 10 on it. The door can't be opened from the outside, for security reasons.

The entrance hall leads to the main staircase, one of the most impressive features of the building. The walls are lined with portraits of past Prime Ministers, with the most recent incumbents at the top of the stairwell and with Winston Churchill on the bottom left.

The Cabinet Room, located upstairs, is separated from the rest of the house by soundproof doors.

This was Cheron's second visit to Number 10. The first time she had noted that the then Prime Minister, Gordon Brown, delivered his speech beside the fireplace. She desperately wanted to say thank you to David Cameron for opening the door of justice to enable King Solomon to walk through. In the hope that David Cameron would use the same spot, she headed towards the fireplace. She was right. She met him and was able to express her sincere gratitude.

It was quite an event. Such a thrill to be able to say, 'yes, we have a faith school in the inner city of Birmingham'. Lots of conversations and lots of useful connections. It was a delight to be able to celebrate in such a way, especially with the rough journey Cheron and her colleagues had had in getting that far.

On Cheron's way out she headed back down those grand staircases alone. She was surprised to see David Cameron casually running up the stairs towards her. He was alone. He had obviously slipped out of the event and was heading back up again. This all felt so surreal to Cheron. Somehow, she sensed he should have been protected – not that she was a danger to him! But surely, he should have had a bodyguard? They both said goodbye as they passed each other on the stairs.

Cheron headed back to Birmingham and to King Solomon with a degree of thankfulness for the school journey so far.

Pastor Doreen Makaya, Lead Chaplain, prays for the school

Revd David Carr, the Order of St Leonard

Extra curriculum activity at King Solomon pushes students out of their comfort zones, building confidence and resilience

Skiing trips provides students with fun and challenging opportunities to engage in exceptional extra-curriculum activities abroad

The official launch of the Excell3 Student Enterprise Bank, a fund to support students business ventures at King Solomon

King Solomon's school building on Lord Street, strategically located within in the Golden Mile of Birmingham

Margaret Thatcher, the longest serving British Prime Minister of the 20th century, hand in hand with Dr Cheron Byfield at an Excell3 event at the House of Lords

Darryl Green, the first boy on the Black Boys Can Project to receive the Lord Bill Morris Award for making rapid progress at school

Some of the first cohort of boys on the Black Boys Can project featured in a transformational aspirational poster in 1999

Sturridge Football Academy students matriculated into King Solomon's sixth form

Two sets of pioneering sisters celebrate the success of Excell3's Amos Bursary scheme. Standing: Baroness Amos and her sister Colleen. Sitting: Dr Cheron Byfield and her sister Audrey

King Solomon, the first school in the country to install and officially unveil the new revolutionary outdoor squash court. World No.5 squash player Sarah-Jane Perry (centre right) and Perry the Bull – the official Commonwealth Games mascot – opened the court alongside England Squash CEO Mark Williams

Foundational members of King Solomon who served faithfully throughout the seven year journey. Left to right: Clive Bailey (Trustee), Carol Brown (Trustee), Dr Cheron Byfield (Founder), Stephen Brookes (senior leader), Revd David Illingworth (Trust Member)

# Chapter Twelve – Valleys

The euphoria of those first days dissipated all too soon.

It had been agreed with the builders that after the opening, for the first few months, the children would relocate back to the portacabins so that work could be completed without distraction.

A few months turned into six months. Six months turned into a year. A year turned into two and a half years.

Parents became disillusioned. This was not what they had signed up for. Stephen was running in circles trying to keep both the builders and the establishment on side with proposed timescales.

But the building challenges had been intensified by another major problem: the recruitment of a suitable principal to lead the school.

## A New Head

The headteacher at the time the school opened, Mrs Fatima, had a lively character and was extremely charismatic in personality. But she was the first to admit she did not have a Christian faith. It was this which caused tension in the school, coupled with what some considered to be her lack of understanding of the cultural background of many within the student body. A number of the parents had sent their children to the school because it was Christian. And with a Christian school, they expected a Christian head.

Mrs Fatima fell out with Mr Hinds, the head of the secondary phase. He no longer wanted to work with her. He resigned.

Bim Oyede, the head of the primary school, became extremely anxious.

'He can't leave, he just can't leave! What's going to happen without Mr Hinds? He's the only one that can manage the Years 7s.'

No school should have to rely on one person to maintain discipline. But being a new school that was growing organically, the school didn't have the resources to employ specialist pastoral staff as yet. That was still part of the future plans. The strong personality of Mr Hinds, coupled with his understanding of the cultural backgrounds of many of the students and the behaviour management strategy that he deployed, had been key to maintaining discipline amongst these lively Year 7s. His approach was very similar to the playbook approach which was to be brought back into the school in future years by a school improvement partner. When he left, many felt that much of the order and discipline also left.

When Mrs Fatima also left, a great deal of effort was made once again to find the right principal for King Solomon. The school needed someone who was a practising Christian and who would commit to the vision. The school emphasis on educational excellence, the development of the character of the student and equipping them to effectively live, work and trade in the global economy was a challenge to any potential principal. But with the failure to appoint comes a certain tension the next time around. After nearly a year of trying, compromises had to be made. An appointment was made.

Let's call the new head, Mrs Mildred.

Mrs Mildred came over well in interview. This would be her first headship, not ideal for a new and complex all-through school, but the school had struggled to find an experienced secondary school Christian head; a challenge which had been exacerbated by a national shortage of headteachers. Mrs Mildred showed confidence and leadership potential for the school and was keen to emphasise that she liked the vision. The board decided to take a chance on her appointment. The establishment were involved in the process. They were happy for her to be appointed. The appointment was made.

Carol Brown had arranged for three sets of interviews – board representatives, a staff panel, and a panel made up of a mix of students. It was the latter panel that raised the alarm.

'Doctor Byfield, she's nice, but she's not the right person! She came over as weak to us, Miss.'

'The children won't respect her, Miss. She won't be able to manage us.'

'And she's not a Christian!' The girl on the panel saying this was a Muslim. Such was the awareness of the need for the leadership of the school to exhibit the faith that was built into the school tenets.

The students were adamant. Mrs Mildred would not be a good appointment. It wasn't that the views of the student panel were being ignored, it was more to do with the fact that no other potentially suitable candidates had come forward. Everyone understood that this appointment was speculative, but there were no alternatives available at this time.

A term had passed, and Mrs Mildred had worked out her notice at her previous school. She was now able to join King Solomon.

The children were in uproar. They didn't want Mrs Mildred. The acting principal called Cheron and asked for her support in dealing with it. Cheron agreed to meet with representatives of the student body and explained why the panel had chosen Mrs Mildred. They were appeased, but not for long!

The second year of the school's existence was well into its stride by the time of Mrs Mildred's appointment. She started working in the portacabins and encountered the ongoing building challenges, alongside some challenging secondary students and parents. Not ideal. Further building delays occurred, reflective of the Grenfell Tower disaster in London. No one would have thought that a fire in London would impact on King Solomon, but it did. The building work had to stop whilst various checks were undertaken to ensure that all the materials used on the building met the required high standards. When the establishment was satisfied, the building work continued.

Maybe if the main buildings had been completed by then, it would have been different. Maybe if parents had been more forgiving regarding the continued portacabins.

Maybe.

## Project Turnaround

The school is located in one of the most deprived wards in the country. An area known for gangs and crime. Many of the students come from challenging and disadvantaged backgrounds.

One of the main challenges at King Solomon School is discipline. There was an urgent need to contain the behaviour of the most challenging students. Some of the staff, like Stephen, had a strong commitment to keeping children in school rather than excluding them. This was contrary to the culture within many schools, and some within King Solomon, who had retained their former school's culture. They saw children with challenging behaviour as problems that should be removed rather than as children with a need for additional support.

Project Turnaround, a new programme to support the most challenging boys in the school, was developed to help with the restoration of students rather than their exclusion. Although it was ready to roll out, there were no spare classrooms in the portacabins to locate it. Some teachers were negative. Many made excuses as to why it couldn't happen.

As Cheron walked around the portacabins, the only space that she could see that could possibly be used for Project Turnaround was a storage room. But this was full. Something had to be done though. Cheron's motto was 'Make it happen!' That's what she did. She called in favours over a weekend from the community. They divided the storage room into two, turning one half into a classroom. Walls were erected.

Doors put in. Carpets laid, chairs and desks put out. Room decorated. Motivational posters put up. All in a weekend and all paid from Cheron's own purse.

Teachers arrived on Monday morning and were amazed. The storage room had been turned around and Project Turnaround could begin.

Reuben was among those boys needing to be turned around. He was on the verge of being excluded. Dr Trevor Adams coordinated the project. Some teachers expected overnight successes. That wasn't going to happen. But successes were to come. For now, it was hard work. Staff like Jemini remained hopeful and committed to the vision. She is known for her mantra: 'When this school sorts out behaviour, it will be an amazing school.'

## Parent College

A Parent College was set up, building on one of Excell3's successful programmes, empowering parents to be effective co-educators for their children. The Department for Education representative was impressed with the concept.

Dr Adams led on this as well. A variety of parent workshops, supporting parents, were to be provided, but behaviour remained the immediate challenge facing the school. This was initially reflected in the work of the Parent College. Parents were crying out for support in parenting their sons with challenging behaviour. Help was now on its way through the college.

Excell3's approach to working with the students and their parents was bearing fruit; slow, but bearing fruit. Dr Adams was getting past the superficial reasons for their sons' challenges and getting down to root causes. It was painful; painful for the boys, painful for the parents, but it had to be done.

## Parent School Partnership

Jean McLeod, a secondary parent, was excited about the school. She used her enthusiasm to set up a Parent School Partnership. Drawing on the support of others, Jean galvanised the parent body to support the school for the benefit and welfare of the children. That was their mission. The Parent School Partnership became very active.

They liaised between classroom teachers and the parents of children in that class, ensuring teachers felt supported. They made sure that the needs of the student body were heard and addressed. They played a key role in the design of the library, creating a quiet oasis for children to sit, read and relax. They gave students an opportunity to occupy the position of a librarian and curator of books while developing customer service and research skills. They hosted coffee mornings. They built on loyal support from local businesses to create a garden for outdoor learning.

Jean, supported by others, raised funds to set up and run a summer school programme for secondary students on coding and robotics. The programme gave the students a head start. They learned how to create their own professional website. It opened their minds to the importance of coding and the role it plays in underpinning many of the jobs of the future.

Jean also initiated an annual careers fair for secondary students. This gave students the opportunity to speak to lots of different employers and gain an understanding of what they offer and the skills needed to be successful in today's economy. It's a great way for students to experience a wide range of businesses in their local community and for businesses to begin to build their talent pipeline.

Several professional parents delivered workshops for King Solomon, drawing on their expertise from their own profession.

The Parent School Partnership had become a positive force within King Solomon.

## The B Classes

Staff complained that Project Turnaround wasn't enough as it only catered for a small number of boys, albeit the most challenging. The stronger, more experienced teachers had their classes under control but the teaching and learning was nowhere near what it needed to be in the classes taught by less experienced teachers. Many more children needed support. The B classes were set up to help these children, again mainly boys.

Although legally compliant, the dull, grey portacabins with uncarpeted floors and with sound travelling from one room to the next, did not provide an ideal learning environment for the students. No wonder the children felt 'this isn't a proper school'. Children described the portacabins as 'tins'. Parents had agreed to this for six months, but when six months turned into over two and a half years, tempers frayed. They felt let down by the establishment.

## Challenging

Despite all the challenges, there were many positive things happening at the school and many of the children loved it at King Solomon.

Martyn Blunt volunteered his time to provide support to some of the more challenging children. Armed with his guitar, he'd engage them in singing. Not the most likely activity for challenging boys. But they did genuinely engage.

As soon as the school was able to appoint specialist pastoral staff, they did so. However, some of the children remained exceptionally challenging. A staff member recommended someone with a track record of dealing with challenging children at other schools. He came. He struggled. He left. A senior pastoral leader was employed. He came. He struggled. He left.

This school was not for the faint hearted!

Ashton Buffong had something special about him. The students respected him. He was not just another pastoral staff member; he was someone who really understood the children. He had been a challenging student himself, so had been in their shoes.

Ashton had success with the B classes. In the longer term, these classes were not the solution to the problem, but it proved to be a good stop gap. At least it gave more teachers the opportunity to teach, and more children the opportunity to learn.

By now, King Solomon was into its third year and the children were still in the portacabins.

Children were continually being sent to the isolation room for poor behaviour. But the isolation room was already full. It was like a conveyor belt. The room was in such high demand, no child could stay in there too long.

Permanent exclusions were always the last resort at King Solomon. Permanent exclusion, particularly for black boys, often meant inclusion into prisons further down the line. Although not always possible, permanent exclusion had to be avoided. Consequently, fixed-term exclusions were high.

And it wasn't just the children that had to be excluded. Some of the parents of rival gangs were getting out of order. They, too, had to be barred from coming onto the school grounds.

## Angry Parents

The secondary school felt the brunt of the massive delays in completing the school building.

The Early Years and primary school continued to thrive. But then they didn't need all the facilities that the secondary students required. Not ideal, but the Early Years and the primary school children could manage a little longer with just one classroom and a good teacher in each. But not the secondary school. They needed their science labs, their IT suite, their language suite, their dance studio, their technical room. Their peers in other secondary schools had these facilities. All schools had them; it was the norm. They were not asking for anything more, just what they were rightfully entitled to. They felt baldly let down by the establishment.

Many parents were tired of attending meetings and being given explanations as to why there was yet another delay. They were tired of being given new dates for the completion of the school building, but they could see how hard the governing body was working on their behalf. They remained excited about the vision, but the delay was impacting on this being realised. Black parents in particular were tired and fed up with being let down by the system.

Parents were not so much interested in who was to blame for the building delays. The builder, the architects, the Education Skills Funding Agency, the impact of the Grenfell Tower fire . . . it didn't matter who it was, all they knew was that their children were not getting access to the state-of-the-art educational facilities they had been promised.

Many lost confidence in the school and were vocal about it at home, in the playground, on social media, as well as in parents' meetings.

Many spoke scathingly about the school in front of their children. This served to engender a culture of disrespect towards the teachers and leaders.

Some parents started moving their children out. Some of the children boasted to their peers that they were leaving. This contributed to further poor behaviour. But many didn't want to leave; they loved it at King Solomon.

Teachers' own dreams and career aspirations had also been challenged. Where were their state-of-the-art classrooms for them to teach from? Where were their science labs for them to conduct science experiments?

Where was the drama studio? Where was the food technology room?

On top of these disappointments, teachers were having to continually deal with angry parents. Parents may be justified in their complaints, but it added to the pressure. Teachers began to resign.

The Education and Skills Funding Council offered to meet with the parents to reassure them that the building works were in hand and to explain that the delays had nothing to do with the school leadership. They asked the contractors to attend the meeting, but they were too afraid to face the parents. They claimed their HR department were concerned about their well-being and advised them not to attend. The Education and Skills Funding Council wouldn't take no for an answer from the contractors. The school directors stepped up too – a number spoke directly to the contractors. The contractors attended. They came out alive.

Throughout this time there were parents, directors, churches and staff praying for the school. Some parents joined the parents' prayer group, others prayed at home, whilst others sought the prayer support of their church. Church groups came to the school and prayed.

Despite the challenges, most of the parents remained professional, patient and supportive throughout this time.

Parents like Charlene Taylor and Kadi Wilson were critical friends and did whatever they could for their school. Having been elected by the parents to serve as parent directors, they worked effectively on the governing body. They built a good rapport with parents and made themselves available to listen and provide appropriate advice. Both were a stabilising force amongst parents.

The Christian ethos of the school was also a key factor in enabling the school to effectively manage the hostile parents.

Many of the black parents historically had a difficult time when they were students themselves, and they brought that history into the school.

They were distrustful of the education system. The chaplains and the culturally competent staff and board members were able to empathise and win parents over. Cheron and other key directors such as Revd Brown and Clive Bailey attended the school regularly to support the leaders and give assurances to parents. Parents grew to trust the school. Over time, there was a huge turnaround in behaviour and attitude.

## The Children Were Right

Within months of Mrs Mildred's appointment as principal the students were joined by voices from the community including politicians and a regulator who contacted Cheron to express their concern about Mrs Mildred's poor leadership of King Solomon school.

The establishment supported the appointment of Mrs Mildred, but the children didn't. 'She won't be able to manage us, Miss.' The children were right. 'The children won't respect her, Miss.' The children were right.

Cheron and her team gave themselves a hard time for not listening to the children. But then, there were no other suitable candidates for the post and the school needed a head.

The board wanted to support Mrs Mildred, but she was not receptive to any proposal for strengthening the leadership, feeling this would undermine her position.

In the end she resigned and wrote letters to the authorities and to many other influential bodies, in an attempt to undermine the board and representatives of the school.

Revd Brown stood in as a temporary principal. He knew the school well. He used to be the chair of the board. Trained in primary education, he did not have the relevant experience for the secondary school, and hence could only be a stop-gap appointment.

Nevertheless, he was able to bring a degree of order to the descending chaos and, with help from his senior leaders and staff, ensure a return to a more disciplined approach to school life.

## Character Development

News about the establishment of King Solomon was beginning to spread across the country. The Evangelical Alliance Education Committee wanted to hear more. They invited Cheron and Stephen to their meeting. The committee listened attentively.

After the presentation, Cheron and Stephen were invited to stay for the rest of the day and join in with a pre-planned seminar.

Unbeknown to them, the theme for the day was character development. Cheron couldn't believe it. Character development was a key part of the vision for King Solomon but until now there had not been a clear framework for it. The Fruit of the Spirit, described in Galatians 5:22 in the Bible, came up time and time again during their discussions. Love. Joy. Peace. Patience. Kindness. Goodness. Faithfulness. Gentleness. Self-control.

This was a watershed moment for Cheron. What better framework to use to develop the character of the children than the values associated with the Fruit of the Spirit? It had been talked about. Proposals had been made. But the seminar confirmed it. Now Cheron had the clarity she needed. Armed with this she headed for the train at Euston Station with a smile on her face and a bounce in her step.

## Fruit of the Spirit

If you walk around the school today, you will hear all about the Fruit of the Spirit. It's a thread in everything. The children are well versed in the language of the Fruit of the Spirit. It's reinforced by staff, parents and the chaplains. In assemblies, it's taught. It's sung – two different versions in fact.

Parents from other faiths were attracted to the school because of the characteristics of the Fruit of the Spirit. A Muslim parent said that this was the decisive factor for choosing King Solomon.

It was easy for the school to embed the Fruit of the Spirit characteristics into UNICEF's Rights Respecting School Award. The school achieved the award quickly.

A few children are appointed as deacons in the primary school. Deacons are outstanding role models within the primary school who make every effort to model the Fruit of the Spirit. They lead in assembles. They lead in prayer. They are little prayer warriors. Whenever they feel the need to pray they will pray.

Cheron and Dr Talburt visited the primary school on one occasion. Towards the end of the visit, one of the boys turned to his fellow students and began to whisper. The whispering spread. The boy turned to Cheron and Dr Talburt and asked, 'Can we sing to you?' They had made an impromptu decision.

Cheron and Dr Talburt said, 'Of course, we'd love to hear you sing.'

The children then burst into a powerful song about the Fruit of the Spirit. They were bold. There was such purity. It was easy to understand why Jesus loves little children.

Cheron's eyes were filled with tears.

# Chapter Thirteen – Sanballat Moments

There were pressures for sure. But so much joy as well, as the school moved on. Staff were excited. Plans were working.

## Constant Battles

There was a constant battle, though, for aspects of the vision to be consistently applied. No more so than the school's specialism of international business and enterprise.

The vision was for students to develop an enterprising mindset, to gain insight into the wealth creation process and develop the attitude, skills and knowledge to be able to spot and capitalise on business opportunities, not just in the UK but globally as well. International business and enterprise was seen as presenting opportunities for equality, equity and as a vehicle out of poverty; a vehicle for upward social mobility and wealth creation.

Some of the leaders paid only lip service to the school's specialism. They didn't understand it or believe in it. Some just wanted King Solomon to be a typical school, delivering the national curriculum and nothing more.

The commitment to the vision that was vocalised at the interview by Mrs Mildred turned out to be mere lip service. At one time business studies, unbeknown to the board, was taken off the curriculum. Parents rightfully complained. But the complaint was made to Ofsted, not to the board. The large donation that Cheron's and Clive's organisation had made to the school to develop a fund and specifically support enterprising students was delayed from being used for that purpose. Mrs Mildred confessed upon leaving the school that she didn't believe in the vision. She considered the pursuit of business and enterprise as unethical and associated with capitalism.

But there were some staff who had bought into the vision and pushed on with it regardless. In both the primary and the secondary school, enterprise fairs had become a regular feature. Children sold products they had created whilst others procured wholesale products and sold them on for a profit.

A full-time post was needed to drive the school's international business and enterprise specialism, but the constant fight for resources meant that when Sean Deer was eventually appointed, it was only a part-time appointment. Nonetheless, he started to make a difference.

## The Solomon Stones

An email popped up in Cheron's inbox. It was from Martyn Blunt. He was sharing an idea he had for a primary monetary system. The primary school would need to create their own currency, which he called 'Solomon Stones'. Students would be rewarded with a Solomon Stone for doing good work. They could use their hard-earned Solomon Stones to purchase goods from the primary school shop.

Martyn provided a detailed proposal of how it would work. It was exciting. The primary monetary system with its accompanying Solomon Shop was officially opened by a representative from the Birmingham Chamber of Commerce. This was a start in developing these young minds to be entrepreneurial. The children loved it. The parents loved it. Cheron loved it. The Chamber of Commerce loved it.

## Daniel's Lions' Den

The International Business Challenge got underway. Students who participated in the challenge and got through to the final stages were invited to face the Lions in Daniel's Lions' Den. This is a similar idea to the BBC's *Dragons' Den*. Students develop their business plans and then make a pitch to a panel of highly experienced business men and women, bank managers and business advisors.

Daniel's Lions' Den took place in the Trust boardroom. The rather impressive room was furnished with a large high-quality boardroom table and chairs, formerly owned by a bank. Although the school paid a fraction of the price for the furniture, the quality helped to create a kind of Alan Sugar type intimidating environment. This was good preparation for the students when they face the real bank manager later in their business life.

### Tyrone – a Budding Millionaire with a Heart of Gold

Tyrone, a Year 10 student with special educational needs, made his international business pitch in Daniel's Lions' Den, where students are challenged to come out alive and thrive. Tyrone articulately and persuasively made his pitch to the panel of business experts. His trade secrets need to be kept but suffice to say his business idea revolved around the use of artificial intelligence to deliver practical business solutions to customers globally, using his own innovative IT platform.

The panel were blown away by the concept. This was not just another good business idea, this one had the potential of becoming a multi-million-pound project. The panel, which included the MD of a well-established IT company, advised Tyrone not to share his business idea with anyone unless he absolutely trusted them, and to get it patented quickly. They advised that he needed a package of wrap-around business and management support, to propel his innovative business venture forward.

Tyrone's business idea was underpinned by an outward facing Christian charitable motive, with profits used to support charities globally. Tyrone was truly a King Solomon student.

Like Richard Branson, who also had special educational needs and was written off by many, Tyrone, to many, was an unlikely candidate to take his position in the business world.

### Sean Deer – International Business Practitioner

Eventually the funds that Cheron's and Clive's organisations had donated to support enterprising students were released. The Student Enterprise Bank could now be launched. The funds would provide interest-free loans to students with sound business ideas to enable them to launch their business venture whilst at school. Cheron and Clive also wanted the school to set up a grant fund to complement the loan fund. The grant fund, the Youth Business Support Fund, would offer small grants to support enterprising students, especially those from economically or socially less advantaged backgrounds, to help them get their feet onto the business ownership ladder. There would be no need for the school to use the funding it gets from the government as the school was in a unique and privileged position to generate its own funds from the annual income it gets from the school's advertising hoarding board, situated next to the school building, as well as income from other school enterprise initiatives such as the King Solomon Shop recently set up.

After a while, the Daniel's Lions' Den International Business challenge became a House Group competition for teams to develop their business ideas, produce a business plan and make a pitch to a panel of business people. Successful teams could apply to the Student Enterprise Bank for an interest-free loan to enable them to turn their business ideas into mini business ventures, with the support of a business mentor. With their profits, students would be expected to treat themselves, reinvest some of it back into their business, tithe by giving ten per cent of their profits to the chaplaincy to support students in need in the King Solomon family, and give some of their profits to a worthwhile cause to demonstrate their commitment to corporate social responsibility. King Solomon was the training ground for the next generation of ethical and socially responsible business women and men.

## More Enterprise Initiatives

Numbers of initiatives were now being driven forward. Plans for the introduction of a student's international business and enterprise passport to capture the enterprising skills of students. Plans for teachers to be trained as entrepreneurial educators. Plans for the establishment of an International Business and Schools Partnership with local, national and global businesses. Plans for international business companies to be linked to each faculty. Plans for a termly International Business and Faith Digest to be produced.

The Student Business Club for the older students would enable students to learn from experienced business people. Clive was keen that all students at King Solomon learn about international business etiquette. In sessions he held with students he advised them:

'When in a foreign country, do as they do. Make sure you have a good working knowledge of that country's business protocols as this will help you to avoid misunderstandings that can jeopardise business. Use the correct titles when making official introductions. In more formal cultures like China and Japan, it's respectful to address a person by their job title followed by their surname. In China, for example, surnames come before first names. When greeting business executives, in some countries you shake hands, in others you bow, and in others you kiss.'


Cheron had been highly instrumental in the development of a Business Incubator Centre in her former job. She wanted to see something similar on offer for the students at King Solomon. A centre that would help young people get through initial hurdles in starting up a business. A centre that would provide fully equipped office units, secure business storage units to store bulk stocks, hot desking facilities and virtual office facilities for those who just need a business postal address and a postal mail service. A centre where young people would have access to networking activities, marketing assistance, high-speed Internet access, help with accounting and financial management, access to finances, comprehensive business training programmes and so much more. King Solomon was in a unique position to set up this provision because it already had three large empty floors. Only one floor would be needed to develop a state-of-the-art Youth Business Incubation Centre. The fifth floor was ideal for the centre with its range of different sized rooms.

There was much excitement about the prospects for King Solomon hosting a national Youth Business Exhibition, with booths in the school hall to showcase students' businesses and increase their customer base.

## Summer School

With the international business specialism a key facet of the school, the school obtained help from many in the business community including Trust member, Dr Adesola. Dr Adesola supported the school in hosting an annual international business summer school. As an international business university lecturer, she travelled over 100 miles from her home to deliverer a number of the sessions. Students were able to learn from top practitioners across a range of fields.

An investment bank offered financial literary classes. A private equity specialist came in to help. Lecturers included a former Rhodes Scholar, *Harvard Law Review* president and investment bankers Goldman Sachs. A strategic partnership was developed with the Massachusetts Institute of Technology, giving students access to expert learning resources. Guest speakers at the business summer school included Omari McQueen, 'Britain's Youngest Entrepreneur' and host of the CBBC TV show *What's Cooking Omari?*

## Recognition

The school was being recognised for its pioneering role in the development of future entrepreneurs. The name of the school – the full name being King Solomon International Business School – was itself gaining interest. Students were encouraged and trained from an early age to develop businesses.

It was possible to walk into a breakout room in the primary school and find seven- and eight-year-olds planning their business ventures. Three girls devising a programme to train the school in first aid with a view to developing a paramedic practice. Three more investigating various online recipes for making soap-bombs with a view to crafting and selling their products at the forthcoming school fair.

Christian business champions and philanthropists were studied. Links with businesses were developed. Well-known business people were invited into the school for lectures, with Christian business ethics being weaved into each initiative.

This was different. It was not a typical approach in schools. Difficult students were responding to the stimulus of business and enterprise and turning their lives around as a result. Youngsters were developing their own business plans and setting out the things they needed to do to achieve it.

Even the uniforms were getting noticed. The bright purple and gold were arresting colours and students were easily identifiable in and around Birmingham as a result, not least as they were often smarter than students from other schools. Andy Street, the Mayor for the West Midlands, even commented on it during a matriculation ceremony, noting how often he saw the smartly dressed students in and around Birmingham.

Support for students who would normally be excluded was also showing some positive results. A good many students were responding well. Not all of them though. Reuben had been in the centre of several discussions with regard to him being excluded for his behaviour. He was seen by some staff as being 'irredeemable' and that it would be best to show him the door, not least because he was a leader and because of the sobering effect that would have on some of the other boys that were associating with him and his behaviour. Dr Trevor Adams worked with Reuben in order to affect change.

Dr Adams encouraged Reuben's creative skills. The building contractors had come up with a design for the school car park and a multi-use games area. Dr Trevor asked Reuben to critique it. Reuben came up with an alternative design solution. Much better that the building contractors' original. The contractors were impressed. Reuben's design won the vote and they used his design.

## Stress Levels

Bubbling under all the success was an ongoing anxiety. The interminable delay in getting into the new building was taking its toll on both staff and students.

As the third year of the school began, the portacabins were still in use, the children still in the car park. Stress levels were high. And now a new cohort of Early Years and Year 7s were arriving into the already packed space. The dining room had to be used for two classes. The corridor was used as another classroom. The staffroom was turned into a classroom. An inflatable dome was erected in the car park for use as a canteen. This wasn't fair on the children. This wasn't what the parents had bought into. Some were patient, others were most certainly not.

Some parents had had enough and, like parents the year before, moved their children to other schools. Others had become very vocal and extremely critical of the school.

Food had to be brought in by outside caterers as there was no room to accommodate in-house catering. The plates had to be sent back, packed away and dirty, as again, there was no room to do otherwise.

Staff needing a place to work were offered a room in the Excell3 offices, a few miles away.

For the more senior students, the lack of resources was affecting their education. They did not have the science laboratories, for example, nor any sports facilities.

It was tough going, especially for the secondary leaders and teachers.


## Bricks

A Christmas card arrived at the school from a parent.

This is what it said:


'In the book of Nehemiah in the Bible, we read that when Sanballat heard that God's people were rebuilding the wall in Jerusalem, he tried every means to stop them. He tried ridicule, then insults. He sent letters to high authorities and then sent in false friends to undermine their plans with diverting comments; comments designed to bring fear amongst the people, hoping to make their hands weak. Nehemiah said, "Don't be afraid of them. Remember the Lord who is great and awesome and fight for your brothers, your sons and your daughters, your wives and your homes."

'He put half to work and half on guard, equipped with spears, shields, bows and armour. They protected the gaps in the wall until they were all filled.'

At the end of the card, the parent wrote:

'Please tell us where the gaps are so we can pray specifically until the bricks are all in place. Brick by brick the wall was built, but they took a lot of flak. We must remain vigilant as we build!'

Remaining vigilant whilst the school is being built has only been possible through God's help and the faithful prayer warriors. Prayer underpins the life of King Solomon. Parents' prayer meetings. Trust members' prayer meetings. Staff prayer meetings. Individuals have engaged in prayer walks around the school. Churches and organisations have prayed.

Just like Nehemiah in the Bible, Cheron and the team around her remained strong. They were to face ridicule, insults, diverting comments and betrayals but they would respond appropriately and continue on the journey to building a successful Christian school.

## Sanballat Letters

The Sanballat letters, letters of complaints to higher authorities, that the parent, Jean McLeod, warned the school about in her Christmas card, constantly landed on the authority's desks. Letters of betrayal, letters that sought to discredit and threaten the survival of the school. Those without the courage to disclose their names sent their Sanballat letters anonymously.

The first Sanballat letter from a former member of staff had brought about a visit from the establishment. The school's funding agreement was at risk. Cheron was being targeted, but the allegations were unsubstantiated. The school was cleared on all issues.

Year after year, sometimes several in one year, Sanballat letters were penned against King Solomon. The school was constantly under attack and subjected to numerous investigations. Cheron was often featured somewhere in these Sanballat allegations. Even when she was out of the country, she was still being falsely accused of things that were impossible for her to have done. The outcome of the investigations was consistently the same – no case to answer. The school was always exonerated.

Revd Brown had been the interim principal for several months and had made a significant impact on discipline. He was a former primary headteacher, a local authority school improvement advisor and a highly respected member of the community. But the authorities were not supportive of his appointment. One of the Sanballat letters led to a visit from the establishment shortly after his appointment. There was no case to answer, but during the officer's visit he learnt about a fight between two children that had taken place the day before. Children fight in most, if not all schools. But a fight between two boys at King Solomon turned out to be cause for an investigation. No, there was no shedding of blood. No injury. The police didn't have to be called. Revd Brown had taken appropriate action and excluded the boys for the day, and the next day they were back at school, restitution made and in their lessons. So why an investigation?

The officer who attended the school requested an internal map of the school and complete access into every part of the building without being accompanied by anyone. It was an odd request and out of line with normal practice, but the school cooperated with the request. What was he expecting to see? The officer later reported back that he had found nothing out of order and commented on how courteous many of the students were.

Every little misdemeanour appeared to be blown up into something it wasn't. Children being taught a 'Golden Text' to memorise a scripture verse (a practice many of their parents were taught at Sunday school) caused the establishment concern. What would be overlooked in many schools came under heavy scrutiny at King Solomon. The authority's overreaction made staff feel that they were being victimised. Inevitably, each investigation resulted in a clean bill of health and no further action, but the investigations were undermining the morale of the staff and creating further unnecessary anxiety on top of the various challenges the school was facing.

There is no doubt that these unreasonable investigations added to the pressure the school felt it was under. And a pressure most schools did not have to face.

# Chapter Fourteen – Build Your School, Lord

Finally.

In April 2018, nearly three years after the school opening, the establishment handed over the keys. Even then, the construction work would not be completed for another year or two. Things were not perfect. The school had to make do with having a temporary wooden gate at the entrance to the school grounds. Everyone needing access to the building had to ring a bell; a member of staff would have to run down the stairs and across the playground to open the gate. Not ideal, but at least the portacabins were a thing of the past. Being in a school building with mainframe heating, double glazing and a hard floor that didn't bounce was like Christmas, Easter and birthdays rolled into one.

The school had been through significant turbulence but had survived. There was much to give thanks to God for. There was to be a lively Thanksgiving Service ahead of term starting.

## Filled

Martyn was playing his guitar as loudly and enthusiastically as he could.

One of the earlier candidates for the principal's post had dubbed the school 'the school that God built'. Since then, others had reached the same conclusion. King Solomon was not just another school, there was something unique about it.

It was with a grateful heart that Martyn, head of primary at the time, began to strum his guitar and sing:

*For I'm building a King Solomon of power*
*And I'm making a King Solomon of praise*

*That will light Birmingham City by My Spirit*

*And will glorify My precious name*

The song is an adaptation of an old favourite Christian chorus by Dave Richards ('I'm Building a People of Power' Copyright ©1977, Kingsway's Thankyou Music).

As Martyn led the procession from the portacabins to the new building, the children filed behind him, all of them joining in with the song. Each was dressed in the new school uniform – royal purple and gold, representing the royalty of a child of God.

Parents were cheering, staff were applauding. Cheron's eyes were filled with tears of joy again. Children were jumping up and down in sheer excitement. One child was consoling her mother who had burst into tears with the thrill and joy of seeing a Christian school finally opening its doors.

High-profile supporters sent encouraging messages. The newspapers reported the success.

Martyn ran over to Cheron in the car park. He had tears of joy in his eyes.

'I'm filled. I just got filled, Cheron!'

After Martyn entered the building after leading the procession, he went to pray. During his time of prayer God filled him with the Holy Spirit.

Although from a traditional Methodist background, Martyn, like the disciples in the Bible in Acts 2:4, couldn't question his experience. God had filled him with His Holy Spirit.

## The Official Opening

The preparations for the official opening of the school were underway. Three years late, but the opening couldn't take place until the school was in its permanent building.

The Church of God of Prophecy had provided office space to the school when the first head, Mrs Fatima, and the team needed somewhere to operate from until the temporary accommodation was ready at the school. The day before the official opening, the school wanted to show their appreciation to the church by giving them a preview of the school before the official opening. The appreciation doubled up as a prayer and praise service. Farm Street Worship Band led that day. Others sang a worship song and De-Andrea Cameron performed a beautiful worship dance.

The discipline challenge within the school had been shared with the church. Prayer was needed. Bishop Neville Fletcher prayed intensely on that day. It was a turning point for the school.

For the opening, Stephen Brooks located a large crown, a fitting symbol for the school. To this day it sits in the reception area of the main building. On that opening day, it was a useful central focus for the ceremony.

Several dignitaries attended the official opening, but it was Mrs Rosalyn Jones, an elderly widow, who was selected to cut the ribbon and unveil the crown. Rosalyn is small in stature and not given to opening schools or anything else really. Her choice as guest of honour was very deliberate. In the Bible, Jesus commends the widow when she gives into the offering at the temple. He tells His disciples that even though she gave just a mite in the offering, it was more than the richest person had given, because unlike them, she had given everything.

Rosalyn Jones had been the first to give towards the school project all those years ago when it first began, and even though the gift had been a small one, it was a significant amount for her. It was very appropriate for her to be opening the building that day. She did a great job!

The school was honoured to have Dr Beverly Lindsay OBE, the Vice Lord-Lieutenant for the West Midlands, as the keynote speaker. She commented on how proud she was that King Solomon was actually birthed.

Dr Beverly Lindsay had caught the vision for King Solomon. She had about twenty years' experience as a school governor, had been chair of governors for an outstanding school and was a highly successful international business trader as well as a practising Christian. She met all the criteria for a Trust member. Cheron broached the question about her joining. Dr Beverly accepted and she's been a valued member.

## Shock

A Department for Education representative called to say they were coming to the school to do a monitoring visit. That was strange. The representative was accompanied by his boss. Strange again. They seemed pre-occupied with Revd Brown. What was he doing there? Why was he the interim principal? It wasn't until the end of their visit that they confessed that they were there because of a complaint. Another Sanballat letter, a letter from a critical persecutor bringing false accusations against King Solomon to destroy the school, had arrived on the establishment's desk. This triggered their visit.

Prior to this, every time the school had a visit from a Department for Education representative, they always left saying to Cheron, 'Cheron, keep going.'

But this time no such words came from their lips. Something didn't feel right.

Two days later, there was a phone call.

It was Ofsted, the schools' inspection body, wanting to inspect the school.

Why now? The school was just moving out of the portacabins. Some of the boxes weren't even unpacked. Children had not yet settled down into their new environment.

Revd Brown was two weeks into his role as interim principal. He was doing a good job in bringing about a return to discipline but there was only so much he could do in two weeks.

Ofsted rated the Early Years as 'good' in all four categories. The primary phase was also deemed to be 'good' on all four categories, although a separate rating in all-through schools is not given and this was lost in the overall report.

Because the secondary phase was rated inadequate, the whole school was deemed to be inadequate and was plunged into Special Measures. Many stakeholders hold the view that the way Ofsted reports on all-through schools is unfair, as their reporting of King Solomon gives the false impression to prospective parents that the primary school was inadequate, which was not true. This affected pupil admissions to primary.

The school being plunged into Special Measures led the Department for Education to threaten to withdraw the school's funding agreement.

## Concert

The stress was lessened by an amazing gospel concert, organised by Ashton Buffong, the pastoral manager. This time the community was invited into the school. The children sang, parents sang. Guest artists included the Birmingham Gospel Choir. Food was on sale during the interlude: curried mutton and rice. The concert was amazing. The final song, 'Total Praise' by Richard Smallwood, summed up the sentiments of how the school felt about God. Children, staff, parents, board members and the community were all in one accord. All up on their feet. Some raised their hands in praise, some bowed their heads in reverence, some rocked, some stood still, but all were praising God.

Against the odds, the school was giving total praise to God. It didn't make sense. Didn't they know the pressures the school was under? Didn't they know they were in Special Measures? Didn't they know their funding was at risk? Yes, they did. But praising God was more important than their circumstances.

People didn't want to go home that night. They didn't want the concert to finish. Non-churchgoers commented, 'If this is what church is like, I want to go to church.'

After the concert Michelle Grannell sent Cheron a photo someone had sent her which captured a rainbow over the school building. God's blessing was on this school. There may be challenges to come, but there was also a belief that God was with them and that He would ensure success. Just as the rainbow was a promise to Noah in the Bible that there would be no more floods, so with the school; they were not going to drown.

## Stabilising Factor

Amidst the Sanballat letters and other destabilising factors, including the numerous Ofsted inspections, there was also a faith inspection. This specifically inspects the faith aspect of the school. As a faith designated school, this is a legal requirement for King Solomon.

Barbara Easton, now the Vice President of the Methodist Conference, is a highly experienced inclusion and interfaith specialist and secondary headteacher. She had supported the Order of St Leonard before the school opened to develop their framework to help drive the Christian ethos of the school. After three years the school was about to face its first faith inspection. How well the school had implemented the framework was about to be tested.

If a school does well in its faith inspection the most it can get is one grade higher than its Ofsted inspection rating. So, in the case of King Solomon the most it could get was an outcome of 'Requires Improvement', unless the inspection deemed the school's faith practices were exceptional. King Solomon had excelled in its faith provision and was deemed by the inspector as exceptional, so was therefore rated two grades higher than its Ofsted rating.

The inspector noted that the emphasis on the Christian faith had been a stabilising factor within the school at a time when things had been challenging:

> 'Since its inception its strong Christian vision has provided a fundamental underpinning to its life and work. It affords consistency amongst the various challenges the school faces. Its Christian service is based on the value of the individual, created and precious to God. This supports the school well in its focus on encouraging pupils' learning alongside the development of their character. This is expressed through a regular focus on the Christian understanding of love, joy, peace, forbearance, kindness, goodness, faithfulness, gentleness, and self-control, summarised as the Fruit of the Spirit.'

The report noted that the chaplains, along with the Christian senior leaders in both the primary and secondary school, had played a significant role in developing the Christian ethos of the school.

**The Fruit of the Spirit**
**King Solomon Values, the King Solomon Way**

The Fruit of the Spirit is the centre and the core
To grow in character this Fruit we just cannot ignore

First we have love, the greatest of them all
Moving unto joy, as we're thankful for the Lord

Peace is a gift from the Prince of Peace
Jesus led by example so we could love with ease

Patience is a virtue which we need to live by too
Kindness toward others, those different and those new

Goodness is a gift from our heavenly Father above
Faithfulness He demonstrated when He sent us His beloved Son

Gentleness was shown when He went to the cross
Self-control was revealed when He laid down His life for us

**Rhema Robinson, aged 9 – Student, King Solomon International Business School**

## Yes, I Am Now!

The Department for Education recommended a consultancy company to support the school. One of the team to come on board was Julie. Julie has worked full-time for Ofsted as an HMI lead inspector and was an advisor for the Department for Education. She was immensely helpful; she knew her stuff. But there was another story too – a personal one.

It was 11.00 at night, one weekend, when an email pinged into Cheron's inbox.

Hi Cheron, I must tell you this!

I had spent many years in the past as a church organist, but I was never a Christian and found myself put off by some of the people I met in church, who were very challenging to say the least!

Just a few days before I visited you, I acquired a new car and my journey to Birmingham was my first long journey. Two hours. The radio seemed stuck on the channel 'Premier Praise' – I thought to myself, oh no, it's one of those Christian radio stations and I don't want this . . . but I couldn't seem to re-tune the radio, so I stuck with it.

And then I visited your school and both you and Matt asked me if I was a Christian; at that point I realised that I couldn't present a reasoned argument one way or another.

I decided that I needed to sort out my own views once and for all. So, when I got home, I went to search for the Bible that had been bought for me in 1979 – a Good News Bible Special Edition. I couldn't find it and my daughter reminded me that I had given her a box of books four years before, that I apparently didn't want, and she had sent them to a second-hand bookshop. I was disappointed because although I didn't really engage with my Bible, it included a lot of maps, pictures, and articles that I thought I'd find useful. That particular special edition had been out of print for many years, but my husband found a copy on eBay, being sold by a second-hand book dealer in Suffolk – apparently the only copy in the country that was for sale. I ordered it – and when it arrived it was my own Bible from 1979, returning home! It won't be leaving me again.

I felt compelled to visit a church and had a truly incredible time – the most faith-affirming experience of my life. So, I am now very glad to call myself a Christian – and I wanted you to know that you played a part in this.

Very best wishes, Julie.

Julie's husband, who had been brought up as a devout atheist, joined her on the faith journey and became a Christian too. They were both baptised in the December of that same year.

## Doomed

The official Ofsted report arrived. Special Measures confirmed. The school's funding was now at risk. It hit the press in December. An article first appeared in *Schools Week News*. It was balanced, but clearly the editor had gone for a killer headline – 'Doomed: The free school facing funding axe'. The word 'doomed' was played with, by showing a picture of the inflatable 'dome' that was being used for the school meals over at the portacabins. It may have been clever mixing 'doom' and 'dome' in the headlines but as a result, all that the main newspapers picked up on was the word 'doomed'.

Parents, already struggling with the length of time it had taken to get into the building, were now even more concerned and several children were moved to other schools. The Secular Society had been running a 'no more faith schools' programme, lobbying government to close them down. This headline was a gift for their social media machine and gave King Solomon further unwanted attention.

The more formal process had also begun. The Department for Education had issued their official notice that they may remove funding. They pointed out that most schools that go down this route do not survive – not the most encouraging of statements. Quarterly meetings were put in place to monitor progress.

## In Everything Give Thanks

Even though Cheron and her team felt like they were in a permanent valley, they refused to give in. It was a hard decision to still go ahead with the end of year annual praise service but they did.

Revd David Illingworth, a Trust member, chaired the event. Whenever he chaired the school's matriculation ceremonies or annual praise services, he always insisted that one of the students co-chaired the event with him. He was highly committed to training young future leaders. It was nearly a two-hour journey for him to travel to the school to host these events, but he made sure he arrived in plenty of time so he could spend quality time getting to know the student that would be co-chairing with him. The impartation of his last-minute words of advice and encouragement had to be done. Today they are presenting to the school and its supporters; later on in life they will be outside the school in the big wide world presenting to businesses, churches, government bodies, locally, nationally, internationally. For David, this was their training ground.

David's strong faith in God was infectious. His confidence was unswerving, nothing seemed to faze him. He looked beyond the challenges faced by the school and saw a mighty God at the centre of the school. He was a tower of strength to Cheron. David was a spiritual guardian of King Solomon. He took his job seriously. This wasn't just another school; this was the school that God built.

Cheron spoke to the students that day:

'As Christians, things don't always go our way – that's not what God promises – but we continue to give thanks.'

And that's what they did. Praises filled the school that day. As Cheron put it, 'In the good times, praise His name, and in the bad times, do the same.'

Mr Dunkley belted out songs of worship in his melodious voice, whilst Mr Yates played skilfully on his guitar. Mr Yates had brought together a King Solomon worship band made up of secondary students. Some sang, some played guitars, some played the drums. Together they offered up high praises to God.

The secondary school presented a dance. And Reuben and his younger brother Micah sang 'Still':

*Hide me now*
*Under Your wings*
*Cover me*
*Within Your mighty hand*

*When the oceans rise and thunders roar*
*I will soar with You above the storm*
*Father, You are King over the flood*
*I will be still, know You are God*

*Find rest my soul*
*In Christ alone*
*Know His power*
*In quietness and trust*

*When the oceans rise and thunders roar*
*I will soar with you above the storm*
*Father, You are King over the flood*
*I will be still, know You are God*
(Words and Music by Rueben Morgan © 2002 Hillsong Music
Publishing)


Remember Reuben? We met him earlier. On the verge of being excluded
for his behaviour. But he survived. And both he and his younger brother
Micah found a Christian faith. Representatives from the school attended
their baptism. It was a joyous occasion to see such transformation. In
doing so, Reuben's attitude radically changed.

And here he was, singing about being still and at peace knowing that
God is God.

There is no doubt that at that moment, the oceans had risen. The
thunder was roaring. But in the midst was a cry of hope. He was still
God. He had got them this far and He could carry them forward. He
was King over the flood. And they – each of them – of faith and no faith,
students, staff, and parents . . . each of them at that moment, as Reuben
and Micah sang, knew that it wasn't over.

There was reason to thank God for the journey so far.

The Fight For Justice

# Chapter Fifteen – The Inner Sanctuary

The school has a chapel *and* a multi-faith room. There you will find the chaplains and those within the school community who are exploring their faith, asking for help, in need of a listening ear or in need of prayer. But the inner sanctuary is not confined to a particular room. The inner sanctuary is anywhere where personal spiritual support can be found. The corridor. The playground. The canteen. Outside of the school. Anywhere.

The chaplains are the main leaders in the sanctuary, although not the only ones, as there are many Christians in the school that make themselves available to provide spiritual support when needed.

Pastor Doreen, the senior chaplain and pastor of a large local church, plays a leading role. Martyn Blunt, originally the head of the primary school, is now known as Brother Martyn, having become a chaplain and brother in the Order of St Leonard. And then there is Chaplain Maureen, another pastor in her own right.

The chaplaincy ensures there is varied worship. They promote the prayer practices of the school and support the school community with developing their faith. They help with activities such as attendance at Christian events and festivals, set up Bible study clubs and provide oversight for community projects.

The chaplaincy also provides a listening ear to those who need it.

Children sometimes find it hard to talk to their parents. They may be struggling in all sorts of areas. The chaplains are there to listen.

Pastor Maureen speaks of helping a child who lost a parent to Covid during the pandemic.

Brother Martyn is on hand to talk confidentially to some of the boys about the pressures they are facing to join local gangs.

There are so many life-affirming conversations.

Discussing with a Muslim girl how best to fast during Ramadan.

Joining in with children from Year 9 speaking excitedly about their new business ventures which they are entering for a national competition.

Another child wanting to show the chaplain his artwork.

Then calling in to a classroom to observe and chat to the students.

On top of that there's the development of global social action, the teaching of Christian business ethics, the help with dedications and baptisms.

## Freedom to Explore

Pastor Doreen enters the classroom. A group of children are doing their school work when out of the blue, one little boy burst out singing a worship song.

'You've learnt some beautiful songs at your church, Jonny.'

'No, Pastor Doreen, I don't go to church. I learnt it here at school.'

'But Jonny, why are you singing in the classroom?'

'I just felt like it.'

Jonny's freedom to sing about Jesus comes from being in a Christian school. It gives him permission to explore and express his faith. At King Solomon, students are free to express what is in their heart, whether through song or through prayer.

On one occasion, one of the primary school boys asked the principal, Revd Brown, if he could pray for him. Revd Brown accepted the offer. The boy placed his hands on Revd Brown and prayed a beautifully affirming prayer.

To have such freedom to express their faith is special, so special.

## Here For You!

One student had several bereavements in his family. Some were violent deaths including shootings. He was streetwise. He was torn. Pastor Doreen counselled him. He wanted to be prayed for. He bowed his head. Pastor Doreen prayed. He finished with tears in his eyes; so, too, did Pastor Doreen. He said thank you and left.

Other streetwise students came for prayer. After assembly, they would wait, look around to make sure all the other children had left the room, then stay behind. They lived in danger zones. Their families were involved in gangs. Their family's lives were in danger. They asked for prayers for protection. Pastor Doreen prayed. They said thank you and left.

The chaplains were also there for those suffering bereavement. One student was so traumatised after a family bereavement she couldn't speak. Pastor Doreen gave her time and space and let her know she could come back whenever she was ready. She came back. She cried. Pastor Doreen cried with her. She asked for prayer. Pastor Doreen prayed for her. She was now ready to start her journey of recovery. She said thank you and left.

## Parents Matter

Weekly parent prayer meetings take place in the school, led by the chaplains. Parents are free to talk about issues and pray and have often testified that they have grown spiritually as a result of attending these prayer meetings.

But the inner sanctuary is not confined within the walls of the school. There have been times when the chaplains are out and about within the community, when parents or students run into them and start talking. In car parks, outside Tesco, outside a pub; chaplains have been known to

174

stop and respond to the prayer needs of parents and children wherever they are.

Parents respect the spiritual standing of the school. They have asked the chaplains to conduct christenings for their children, wanting their children to be dedicated in the school.

Despite being in Special Measures and having a Termination Notice hanging over it, parents still choose to send their children to King Solomon because of its strong Christian ethos and the spiritual care available for the children. Seeing a child in distress being prayed for in the corridor during a visit was the decisive factor for one of the parents in choosing King Solomon.

## Staff Matter Too

On one occasion Pastor Doreen felt prompted to go to a particular classroom. Upon arrival she discovered that the teacher in the room had an ongoing serious diagnosis after having had chemotherapy just the week before. The teacher was preparing to start the lesson in half an hour's time. They talked. They cried together. They prayed. The teacher dried her eyes and welcomed the children into the classroom.

On another occasion Pastor Doreen walked into a room full of support staff. They shared and talked openly about their experiences of war in their home country. They had escaped. They were refugees. And they were so grateful to have found employment.

Staff will seek spiritual support from the chaplains to help deal with some of the challenges they face with the children. Many of the staff have never worked at a school before where there are so many families with social problems. They find comfort and strength in having someone to talk to which adds a different perspective to the one their line manager would typically give.

Support does not just come from the chaplains. It can come from staff as well. Michelle Grannell describes a time when she had found herself in a challenging situation and a member of staff came up to her and said, 'I'd like to pray for you.' This happened just at the moment when she needed it. Michelle went away feeling uplifted and more prepared to deal with the challenges.

At times, spiritual support can come from the parents too. Michelle recalls a time when she was in hospital suffering with Covid-19. Parents sent her recordings of songs and of messages, saying that they were praying for her. God sustained Michelle during those troubled times.

## Staff Challenged

But King Solomon is not just a place for support; it's also a place for spiritual growth, where a Christian's faith is challenged.

Christian staff have learnt that when God is in control He can use whomever He wants to use whenever He wants to. They have seen people whom they least expected, colleagues without a faith, buying into and propelling the vision of the school.

Pastor Doreen felt God challenged her faith to send her own daughter to King Solomon. One of her famous sayings is 'without a test there is no testimony'. And now Pastor Doreen was being tested. Amidst the negative publicity about the school, did she really believe that King Solomon is an excellent school, a place where God is present? She was challenged to prove it. She did. She put King Solomon down as her first-choice school for her daughter. No regrets. Her daughter is doing well.

Michelle Grannell was challenged to apply the Fruit of the Spirit teaching to all aspects of her own life. She couldn't just teach it, she had to live it too.

A lasting and memorable moment for Pastor Doreen was when she was asked to support a mother who needed help to inform her daughter that her best friend had just died. Pastor Doreen made herself available. Breaking the news to a girl who came in to see her at one moment happy and smiling wasn't easy, but it had to be done. The girl cried. Pastor Doreen cried with her. She helped the girl to understand that her friend had gone to heaven.

Pastor Doreen was humbled by the girl's childlike faith, accepting what the Bible said. Pastor Doreen encouraged the girl to write a goodbye letter to her friend. She did. It was honest, so open, so trusting. The girl said she would rather have died herself and taken her friend's place. The childlike love and compassion she showed reflected her faith in Jesus. It was a lesson to Pastor Doreen. She grew in faith herself. That little child led her into areas of understanding of her own faith she had simply not comprehended before.

**Gentleness**
**A King Solomon Value, the King Solomon Way**

Gentleness is passive
Above all things, it's submissive to God's will
It often takes the form of meekness
And it allows one to be still
It exercises wisdom and assists in appeasing sorrowful souls

But gentleness is also aggressive
It removes harshness
It dismisses folly
It strangles difficulties

And it wrestles for serenity

**Yahanna May – Excell3 Intern**

## Other faiths

King Solomon has from its inception, given due regard to those from other faiths and no faith.

King Solomon worked in partnership with other organisations, such as the Faith & Belief Forum, as well as schools from other faiths. These partnerships enabled students to participate in multi-faith events and deepen their knowledge and understanding of other beliefs.

Within the school, King Solomon developed a dedicated multi-faith room. Initially when the multi-faith room was established there were scheduled times for its opening. After a while the chaplains made the decision to keep it permanently open so students, staff and parents could gain access to the room as and when they required. This has been particularly helpful for students of the Muslim faith who want to pray at certain times.

The chaplaincy finds time for everyone, whether they are Christians, of another faith or have no faith. For them it isn't about telling students that they have to believe the Bible, it's about talking to them and listening to what they have to say. Pastor Doreen held regular Bible clubs. After a while the club turned into a drop-in centre for students who wanted to talk about faith; any faith. It started to attract a lot of Muslim students. After a while the club changed from a Bible club to a faith club in response to the needs of the children.

Popular discussions have centred around subjects such as the Koran and the Bible; the similarities and the differences.

Students discussed standards of dress, and what is acceptable.

They talked about the discipline of prayer. The chaplains always ensure that permission from parents is granted before children take communion or receive a blessing. On one occasion they were serving communion. During the service a student from another faith came to take communion. They explained what the wafer and wine represent, then asked if her parents would allow her to take communion. The girl opened up and said she wanted to be a Christian. They listened to her but refused to give her communion without her parents' consent and prayed a blessing instead.

The girl later did become a Christian. God gives everyone a free will; this is to be respected. Just as Jesus doesn't force anyone to become a Christian, neither does the school. The school didn't coerce or push the girl into becoming a Christian; it was her choice.

## Atheists

King Solomon is there for the atheist too.

A secondary student, a declared atheist, approached Pastor Doreen for a chat. Despite his declaration as an atheist, he wanted to come to a Christian school. Pastor Doreen quickly realised he wasn't looking for doctrine and biblical scriptures, but rather he wanted to see the real live Jesus portrayed and embodied in Christian attitudes and lives. It was in the sanctuary that he felt at liberty to share his thoughts and have the confidence that he would be listened to. He later chose to take part in collective worship and read scriptures.

## LGBT

Students and staff professing to be LGBT or claiming to be confused about their sexuality have found refuge in the inner sanctuary. The chaplains make time for them; for everyone. Some were experiencing emotional pain and anguish, but the chaplains were overwhelmed with a sense of compassion for each of them. Their first port of call was always to find out what the person's needs are and how Jesus can supply that need.

One of the LGBT members of staff explained that this was the first time in her life she felt able to talk about her sexuality. When she eventually left the school, she raised funds for the school and posted a cheque to Cheron.

## Lascars

Ralph Turner wrote a blog about Lascars, a term which died out in the 1950s. Lascars are people rejected and abandoned by their mother country and their original society but, at the same time, they have not been adopted by their new culture either. Abandoned and rejected, they live on the outside of both their original culture and their adopted one. Abandoned by one and rejected by another.

For the chaplains, King Solomon is a place where the abandoned and rejected are restored! Pastor Doreen talks about a Lascar she met just days after receiving Ralph's blog.

'Today a "Lascar" approached me at lunch time, most unexpectedly. A little thing, Year 7, not the most popular, but she separated herself from the crowd and asked me to play the song "No Longer Slaves" which talks about not being a slave to fear because of the relationship we have with God. I played it at full blast – she stood alone in the crowd and sang along to the song. When she'd finished, she returned to say thank you. *She left with a glow.*'

King Solomon is here for the Lascars as well.

## Wicca

A student had taken on the belief and faith of her mother and was involved in séances, yet here she was in a Christian faith school.

The first thing the chaplains recognised was that she is a human being first and foremost. The girl had left her previous school because she wasn't getting on well there. She had needs and had come to King Solomon. She was crying out for help. The priority for the chaplains was to demonstrate the love of Christ to her.

People have a perception of how Christians respond to things like this. For example, putting up the sign of the cross, throwing holy water and saying three hail Mary's! But the chaplains did not respond in these ways. Neither did they become doctrinal, saying 'thou shalt not'.

What the student experienced was Christian love and compassion for her as an individual. Her fellow students were not afraid to challenge her. In fact, it was the children that talked amongst themselves. They respectfully challenged her to look at her practices from a biblical perspective.

**Faithfulness**
**A King Solomon Value, the King Solomon Way**

Who is faithful like the Lord?
Can anyone fill the cavity in our hearts and seal us with such grace and compassion?
As sure as the ocean roars, as sure as winter precedes spring, as sure as the dew kisses the fields – so is His faithfulness to us.
New every morning are His mercies.

To think that such a mighty God sings over me – my feeble soul yearns for His love.

How dare I stray, wonder away, from the gracious path that He has ordained for me,
Leaving the fold like a wondering sheep, He lovingly draws me into His everlasting arms, there I find refuge – freedom, liberty.

Who is utterly trustworthy? Knowing my deepest thoughts, my darkest stains yet still presents me faultless, before the throne of grace? His unchangeable commitment to me, artistically demonstrated – a bow in the sky – a reminder of His covenant dedicated to me.

Who else can I lean on? Completely dependable, the rock of all ages, yet still the lamb that was slain.
A firm foundation in a world on which I cannot stand, rooted as a tree by the rivers of water
I place my feet firmly, I remain unshaken.
He will never let me down, He will never let me fall.

Promise keeper! Loyal saviour!
Just as He is dependable, reliable for me, I strive to mirror His ways – return them as a gift – back to Him.
As the deer pants for the water, I long after you. Growing in you, leaning not on my own understanding.

I must stand in the face of adversity.
I must stand when others forsake me.
I must stand unmovable in the face of compromise.
I must stand when all seems lost . . .

For who is like our faithful Lord?
No . . . Not one.

But as a child resembles its parents
We His children who remain connected to His vine
Will grow to become faithful, trustworthy and dependable with time.

**Dionne Rey – Teacher, King Solomon International
Business School**

## Social Action

The children are taught not to be SELF FISH. Love and kindness are key values of the Fruit of the Spirit and this has to be lived out in seeking to meet the needs of others.

Involvement in social action is an integral part of the school's life. Staff and parents are also encouraged to get involved in the school's social action initiatives. Its social action motto is 'a school in the heart of Birmingham which reaches out to its local community, its nation and its world'.

The school itself is modelling the behaviours it is seeking to develop in the students. There is support for fair trade. The Solomon Shop, the school's official shop, sells fair trade products, thus supporting products that are grown, produced, and sold under a system that guarantees that farmers and agricultural workers are paid fairly for their work.

The school also gets involved in lobbying and campaigning. They lobbied Birmingham City Council for funding for highway safety measures outside the school. They got involved in the red box campaign collecting and distributing sanitary products for pupils.

In recognition that charity begins at home, the Parent School Partnership have focused their social action initiatives on solutions to problems within the school. Some families struggle to buy school uniforms. In response to this, the Partnership initiated recycling school uniforms that are in good condition, to support pupils from low-income families.

Students reflect the school's values in their local community. One of the secondary students, unbeknown to him, was spotted helping an old lady in the local community. This was captured on Facebook and over 30,000 people followed the story. The student was surprised – the school not so much. These kinds of actions happen all the time. Students learn to care, to think about others. And it shows.

Students volunteer their time to support established community groups such as the Birmingham City Mission homeless project and food bank, as well as organising their own school-based food bank. In association with school contractors, they have provided food hampers for numerous families during the holiday seasons and have filled a backpack with supplies for people who are homeless.

The school choir regularly visits care homes bringing hope and cheer to the residents.

Students raised funds to host summer school programmes to provide confidence-building courses for girls over a four-week period. The initiative was covered on the ITV news as they provided free 'back to school bags' for about 100 pupils having received donations from local businesses and the community.

The school's commitment to social action also extends abroad. Fundraising initiatives takes place to support a partner school in Ghana, West Africa, and to sponsor a foster child in another country. More and more opportunities are being afforded to help students develop empathy as well as important skills such as problem solving and conflict resolution in the community.

## Cultural Capital

The school aims to help students with what it calls its 'cultural capital'. Special Saturday morning extra-curricular activities are known as Super Saturdays at King Solomon. Students attend this session with high expectations of being taught something new and exciting that they don't get during normal school lessons. It's during these Super Saturdays that students are equipped with tools to be able to function effectively amongst the more affluent in society.

One Saturday, students attending a session on etiquette were faced with a full banqueting table as they walked into the room. This was part of a special presentation from Reuben Lynch, an award-winning black professional toastmaster. He covered a range of etiquette topics including modern manners and social etiquette, meeting new people, introductions and greetings.

Students were taught about proper posture and keeping elbows off the table, how to use cutlery, comparisons with other countries... These may sound small and unimportant but modern manners can be the difference between success and failure in the business world.

Weeks afterwards students were still talking about how surprised they were to learn that when fine dining, they should break their bread, not cut it, and that they should spoon their soup away from themselves. Some of the girls are particularly fascinated by the insight they gained into the diverse international eating styles. They all came away with an acute awareness of the importance of proper etiquette and of how essential this is for making a favourable impression not only at certain types of social occasions, but at business events.

Cheron also wants the students to have elocution lessons so that they develop the skills to be able to speak the Queen's English, and culture-switch whenever they need to. This is precisely what some of the black male students in her research study in USA universities were able to do so effectively. They held onto their racial identity, so were able to speak in their racial dialect, but were able to culture-switch and speak the Queen's English when they needed to, using more acceptable pronunciation, grammar, style, and tone.

## School Environment

The Christian ethos of the school is evident from the moment a visitor enters the grounds. The reception area contains a large rolling screen which reflects the Christian life of the school. Assemblies. Choirs singing. Matriculation ceremonies with children being prayed for. The chaplains standing in unison.

There are strategically placed Christian symbols – crosses, crucifixes and other Christian artefacts – in classrooms and around the school which act as a daily reminder of the school's Christian heritage and provide further opportunities for personal reflection.

Background Christian music can be heard in the entrance hall, hallways and in the dining room; both traditional and contemporary music reflecting the multi-denomination Christian ethos of the school.

Inspirational scripture quotes are seen throughout the school. The chapel contains artwork and objects conducive to a sense of awe and wonder linked to Christian values.

Let's introduce you to a couple of the girls. Maybe we'll leave their names out for obvious reasons! This morning they had a bit of a shouting match. Not quite a fight, but enough to find themselves in the Grace Inclusion Centre. An hour later you will find them together in one of the safe spaces in the school. This includes the school chapel and the multi-faith room. These are spaces where students can take time out to be quiet and think, pray, read the Bible, consider their own feelings and their relationship with others, especially their place in God's world. Typically, staff will ask students to sit and discuss any issues with the person they have offended or been offended by.

Another hour on and the girls are back in class and sitting next to each other.

There is no doubt that the Christian ethos helps with this kind of reconciliation. It can be summed up in the Nicene Creed which is a tenet of the school's faith. This is clearly displayed in the school chapel:

*We believe in one God, the Father, the Almighty, maker of heaven and earth, of all that is, seen and unseen.*

*We believe in one Lord, Jesus Christ, the only Son of God, eternally begotten of the Father, God from God, Light from Light, true God from true God, begotten, not made, of one being with the Father; through him all things were made.*

*For us and for our salvation he came down from heaven, was incarnate from the Holy Spirit and the Virgin Mary and was made man. For our sake he was crucified under Pontius Pilate; he suffered death and was buried. On the third day he rose again in accordance with the Scriptures; he ascended into heaven and is seated at the right hand of the Father. He will come again in glory to judge the living and the dead, and his kingdom will have no end.*

*We believe in the Holy Spirit, the Lord, the giver of life, who proceeds from the Father and the Son, who with the Father and the Son is worshipped and glorified, who has spoken through the prophets.*

*We believe in one holy catholic [universal, not Roman Catholic] and apostolic church.*

*We acknowledge one baptism for the forgiveness of sins.*

*We look for the resurrection of the dead, and the life of the world to come.*

*Amen.*

# Chapter Sixteen – Shadows

*Even though I walk through the valley of the shadow of death, I will fear no evil, for you are with me.*

The words of Psalm 23 rang out in Cheron's mind as she opened the door to her office. Special Measures. Parents taking their children out of school. Staff leaving. A 'Minded to Terminate' notice.

But it's a *shadow* of death, not death itself. The school was still alive. There was still a hope and a future for it.

A big sigh. A sip of coffee. Computer turned on. And a new day ahead.

New challenges for sure. But God is greater.

## Temporary Head

Revd Brown began that arduous task of beginning to turn the school around, whilst he was the interim principal.

It was important to get the right headteacher. Pastor Doreen gathered a few others and together they prayed throughout the whole week leading up to the interviews. It was time well spent.

After a false start with a possible joint appointment, there were no other clear candidates in the interview bar one. Miss King had good secondary experience but lacked a Christian faith. A decision was made to appoint her to a temporary head position – and it turned out to be an inspired decision. With her positive and can-do attitude, the school started to make progress.

Miss King started working on a voluntary basis even before her official appointment.

Initial concerns from some, mainly due to the lack of a Christian faith, began to dissipate as Miss King demonstrated a genuine commitment to the school and the children. She was respectful to all board members, the parents, staff, and the children. She was a strong leader. She challenged appropriately and supported appropriately. She was professional with a strong commitment to equality. So much so, that when she eventually left everyone was sorry to see her go.

Within a week of her arrival, the school was buzzing. There was an increased sense of purpose, staff felt assured that they were being listened to, and goals were revisited and revised. The excellent work Revd Brown had done, especially in discipline, was built upon further.

## Sleeping Giant

For Cheron, Miss King's appointment came as a relief after the hard times. Here was someone who understood the overall vision for the school; the work to include and not exclude; the promotion of enterprise. It was all there, all recognised, all supported.

The original vision documents were revisited and put into a vision-map, setting out how each statement could be turned into reality. The school's aims and purposes were brought to life, and then applied by each leader to their own curriculum area.

And not only a re-casting of the vision and purpose – a re-casting of key staff as well. Some were let go, others brought in, others promoted. Staff contracts were reviewed to ensure equity. This didn't always go down well for some staff, but it had to be done. Miss King was bold, not afraid to challenge and uncaring as to how she herself was perceived so long as the school benefited from the changes.

Unlike some of the former principals, Miss King didn't pretend to be a Christian, but she did show a high degree of respect for the Christian ethos of the school. She respected the chaplaincy. She went out of her way to regularly consult with Pastor Doreen and the chaplaincy team about new initiatives before she implemented them.

Another proof of Miss King's work was in the response from parents. A number who had strong reservations about her appointment became her biggest supporters. They saw the changes, the improvements, the way she related to the children, the parents and board members and the increased enthusiasm to learn within their own children.

She loved the children and the children loved her, especially those in primary.

In the end, though, it was only a temporary appointment. But Miss King described King Solomon as being special, a type of school that she had never come across in all her years in education. She described the school as a sleeping giant and advised the school to wake up and put themselves on the map.

## Cyrille Regis Hall

The Order of St Leonard's annual praise service was always an important event in the school, coming as it did at the end of the academic year. Despite the pressures, there was much to give thanks for, not least because the school had been successful in its fight to have its own assembly and sports hall. The contractors had argued that the school didn't need a sports hall because they could use a nearby facility. But Cheron insisted. In addition to needing a sports hall, like most schools, King Solomon is a faith school, so it needed an assembly hall to host collective worship, its praise services, and its matriculation. It's a business school so it needed a hall to host business fairs and exhibitions as well as careers fairs. It's a community school, so it needed a hall that it could let out to the community.

The praise service of July 2019 coincided with the opening of the much-delayed assembly and sports hall, which the school named the Cyrille Regis Hall, in recognition of the late West Bromwich Albion and Aston Villa footballer. Cyrille had been a keen supporter of the school and had a strong Christian faith. His family attended and Julia, his widow, opened the hall. Revd David Carr from the Order of St Leonard delivered a highly inspirational keynote speech, not surprisingly, given that his own background was as a former football manager.

Kesia, the head of the sports department, led the celebrations of King Solomon students' sporting achievements. Students had been excelling in many areas. They won gold in the Aston Indoor Athletics School Games. Many had seized opportunities to go on the school's skiing trips to Bormio, Italy. Some primary students who excelled in sports played for the District Football Team, the West Bromwich Albion Basketball Club, and competed in Jiu Jitsu competitions.

The school was soon to welcome the ex-Liverpool footballer Daniel Sturridge's Football Academy, into its sixth form; a development that the late Cyrille Regis would no doubt applaud. Students were also to become sports leaders, helping to lead and deliver a Sunshine Festival event for over 40 primary pupils across Aston.

This particular praise service was also used to give recognition to all the volunteers that had given their time to support the school.

Miss King was recognised for the service she had given to the school on a voluntary basis before she became the temporary head. Her parting words were, 'I have loved working at this school. And if, in five years' time, I have found a Christian faith, I would love to return as your principal.'

She left the school with a Bible, a gift from the board, and remains a friend of King Solomon.

But, with her departure, shadows were beginning to fall again. The recruitment for a permanent head continued.


## Deeper Shadows

Suffice to say, it didn't go well.

The recruitment process produced no outstanding candidates. But the school needed a principal. Cheron successfully negotiated a two-year secondment with a local school for a Christian deputy head to take on the role of principal with mentoring support from the head. This was an arrangement that the school itself had benefitted from in the past, and it worked well.

But then the unexpected call came at the eleventh hour. The school had to pull out because their own staffing challenges arose, and they no longer could afford to release their deputy.

This created increased pressure. Time was now against King Solomon.

Word got out that King Solomon was looking for a principal. June approached the school. She had been out of headship for a while and wanted to get back, so was readily available. King Solomon needed a head, ideally someone who could start at short notice. A perfect match. Or was it?

## Disaster Zone

Early signs caused concern. Even before June's employment commenced, she showed a lack of interest in the school to the point that those who had been on the recruitment panel began to question whether she really wanted the job.

Within the first week of her starting concerns were raised.

The students who met her felt she didn't like them and not many warmed to her. Teachers complained about her lack of interest in students and in the staff. Even after three weeks at the school, some students remained unaware that she had started work.

Things got worse. As news got out that June was working at King Solomon, staff from her former schools started providing negative feedback about her. The feedback corroborated some of the concerns King Solomon had. This served to confirm that she was not the right fit for this particular school. There was a fundamental clash of values. Standards in the school began to deteriorate. Increasingly more serious concerns were coming to light.

But Ofsted was due any day now. If the Ofsted outcome was poor the school was at risk of closure. The Year 11s needed a head that was going to drive them to do their best in their impending exams.

An emergency board meeting was called.

The board deliberated at length. This was tough. They were caught between a rock and a hard place. The board agreed that this wasn't the right school for June and she was not the right head for King Solomon.

A Moses-basket decision had to be made – a decision between two very high-risk options.

## A Moses-Basket Decision

Jochebed, the mother of the biblical character, Moses, knew that antagonists were out to kill her baby. In response, she was faced with two high-risk options. Option one was to bury her head in the sand and wait for the antagonists to kill her baby, hoping they may pass her by. The second option was to try and save the baby by putting him into a basket and sailing it down the crocodile-laden river in the hope that Moses would survive somehow. She chose the latter. So into the basket Moses went. Moses survived.

Now the King Solomon board was faced with its Moses-basket decision. They had to choose between two very high-risk options. Option one was to bury its head in the sand and wait for the school to come crashing down. Alternatively, to let June go and recruit someone who was committed to the school and to improving the Year 11 results. But this option was dangerous. They would have to face the wrath of Ofsted and the Department for Education. They chose to act in the best interest of the school and the Year 11s, knowing full well what the potential consequences could be. They prayed, put the matter in the hands of God, trusting God that somehow, like Moses, the school would be rescued. They stood united. June had to go. June did not take the decision well. Unexpectedly she handed in her keys and walked out.

To make matters worse, a number of the secondary senior leaders resigned. Other staff resigned. Primary senior leaders, Mrs Kent and Mrs Grannell, had to take over the running of the school with Mrs Kent acting as the accounting officer. They stepped up to the mark. They were brilliant. The board began the recruitment for an interim head and for secondary leaders.

Many were convinced that the school was doomed to fail. This extreme turbulence took place just before an Ofsted visit.

Then the dreaded call came from Ofsted.

The outcome was inevitable. A damning monitoring report.

But Clive and Carol, both on the board, remained strong in their faith. Repeatedly Clive would say. 'It's not over till it's over.' David Illingworth remained a tower of spiritual strength, constantly sharing encouraging words from the scriptures.

## The Shadows Pushed Back

Jill Saunders sat on the board of directors; she was very knowledgeable and supportive. She introduced Cheron to Mrs Abrahams, a recently retired headteacher who Jill thought might be up for the challenge.

A meeting followed and Mrs Abrahams agreed to a six-week temporary headship role. She got stuck in straightaway and began to make improvements. She loved the school. So much so, she applied for the substantive headship role and was successful, making a long-term commitment to the school.

Jill Saunders recommended another name to work alongside Mrs Abrahams. Mrs Popratnjak. The same head that had been at College

High all those years ago. Mrs Popratnjak had recently been awarded an MBE for turning around a failing school and agreed to work alongside Mrs Abrahams on a consultancy basis.

Both women were Anglicans with a strong Christian faith.

With their appointments things began to get back on track.

## One Stop Christmas Outreach

Cheron received a WhatsApp message which had gone viral. It was of children singing in the One Stop Shopping Mall. They were impressive. When she looked closer, she saw it was King Solomon primary children singing live in the busy shopping centre. Cheron was taken aback. Mrs Kent and Mrs Granell had taken the primary school choir out of the school walls and onto the streets. People were amazed. Their uniform was an eye catcher and their young voices melodious. Their Christmas shopping centre concert was a lively success. They were singing their little hearts out. Crowds gathered. Shoppers stopped. People watched. Many joined in.

Dionne Rey and Sharmaine King were amongst the staff directing the choir. There could be no better choir conductors than these teachers who are worship leaders in their own churches.

The shopping centre was filled, not with songs such as 'Jingle Bells', but with young voices singing of Jesus' birth, death and resurrection. Singing songs of praise and thanksgiving. Singing songs of hope. Singing the Tasha Cobbs song 'You Know My Name':

*He knows my name*

*Yes, He knows my name*

*He knows my name*

*Yes, He knows my name*

*And oh, how He walks with me*
*Yes oh, how He talks with me*
*And oh how He tells me*
*That I am His own . . .*

*And oh how you comfort me*
*And oh how you counsel me*
*Yet it still amazes me*
*That I am your friend*

*So now*
*I pour out*
*My heart to you*
*Here in*
*Your presence*
*I am made new . . .*

*No, no fire can burn me*
*No battle can turn me*
*No mountain can stop me*
*Cause you hold my hand*

*And now I'm walking in your victory*
*Cause your power is within me*
*No giant can defeat me*
*Cause you hold my hand*
(Written by Brenton Brown & Tasha Cobbs Leonard. © 2017

Meadowgreen Music Company, Tasha Cobbs Music Group, Thankyou Music administered by Capitol CMG Publishing, Integrity Music Ltd.)

The singing echoed through the shopping mall. The shoppers were reminded that they are personally known to God, that He knew them by name, and wants to be their friend.

Whilst some shoppers tuned into the more slower tempo song 'Be Still and Know That I am God', others were rocking and clapping to Hezekiah Walker's song 'Every Praise'.

Their singing had become infectious. The children were praising God. The crowds were praising God too. A passer-by had heard the children singing from a distance and said they sounded like angels.

Cheron was so proud of these bold little children. Proud of their confidence in praising God in public.

## Grace

During the storms, a calm oasis had been created in the centre of the school. If you walk up the stairs to the second floor, you will find to this day, an inclusion zone, appropriately named the Grace Inclusion Centre. It is the physical result of the planned strategy of the school to support rather than exclude troubled students.

There you will meet a secondary school teacher, Kesia. She has left her rural Buckinghamshire for the challenges of the inner city. Staff at the Grace Inclusion Centre talk of the need to see that failure is never a person, but always an incident. And as they comment, 'God never created a failure.'

With the use of physical props, students are helped to see what has happened and how to recognise the signs again; what staff call 'catching the emotion' before the emotion catches you.

Kesia expresses her excitement at the success of their sports department, an area she also heads up. The school came third out of eighty schools in a recent football competition. Some of the more challenging boys have found success in football and have been signed by local clubs, including the Premier League club Aston Villa.

In the next room, on this virtual visit, you will find Michaela, working with asylum seekers, helping them get a grasp of the English language. Michaela started as a volunteer, then trained as a teacher and now runs this section of the centre. The enthusiasm is palpable. The results are self-evident.

The challenge is a real one. Challenging children. Challenging parents and carers.

The school inspector had noted how the Christian ethos and the Fruit of the Spirt had its impact on attitudes, behaviour and learning. The various elements of the Fruit of the Spirit are well articulated by pupils and staff, including that of self-control.

**Self-control**
**A King Solomon Value, the King Solomon Way**

When I have lost my temper
I have lost my patience too
I am never proud of anything
I angrily do

When I have talked in anger
And my cheeks are getting red
I've always muttered something
Which I wish I'd never said

I think having self-control
Is trying to be wise
And not doing bad things
Of which I have to apologise

**Ava-Rae Howell, aged 9 – Student, King Solomon International Business School**

Walk through the Grace Inclusion Centre doors and you will find a calmness in each of the rooms. A real sense of love and support with the aim of helping the student get back into mainstream school as quickly as possible with all the support that he or she needs.

'Going the extra mile' is a Christian term of course. It is exemplified by the way staff seek to keep students in school – even when they run away! Some have been involved in the County Lines drugs rings. This is the trafficking of drugs into rural areas and smaller towns, away from major cities such as Birmingham. Traffickers recruit vulnerable children, including children in referral units or those who have been excluded from school, as drug dealers.

Ashton Buffong has seen a number of these cases. On more than one occasion, he has taken time off school, sometimes taken as holiday, to follow a lead and bring a child back to school and back to their family.

And the children do respond. Look at Prince. He decided to move away from the troubled path he was heading down in a dramatic way. One day he put himself in the corner of a room in the Grace Inclusion Centre and surrounded himself with tables and chairs, barricading himself in. It was a physical declaration of a decision he had made. He said he had decided to 'fix up', to transform his ways. He would no longer live as he had been doing. He would study. He would change. He has changed. He later went on to be selected to work alongside Dr Trevor Adams as co-chair of a Parent College conference at the school. He left school with 11 good GCSEs.

It is called the Grace Inclusion Centre for a reason.

## Student Awards and Commendations

The Grace Inclusion Centre was rescuing children. And the school as a whole was challenging the children. They were rising to the challenge. They entered the West Midland Regional Theatrical Competitions and fought off some strong competition. They received commendations and awards for their theatrical performances from the Lord Mayor of Birmingham in the presence of the Knights of St Columba and other dignitaries at the Council House Chambers.

Some entered the UK maths challenges and were successful in obtaining certificates. Two students were amongst the top percentage of students nationally.

Students seized the opportunity to participate in the iRail Challenge at the National College of High Speed Rail (HS2). Here they were mentored by industry experts, visited several rail-related sites in the city, met local companies and participated in the bridge building challenge. Their design passed the judging panel tests and they were awarded a finalists' certificate.

## Emergency Meeting

Cheron had major surgery planned and was still recovering when the Department for Education emailed her asking for a meeting. It was not a surprise. The Moses-basket decision had been made. Now the school had to face the consequences.

With Cheron on sick leave, Carol Brown, the vice chair, deputised for her.

There was an expectation that the Department for Education would be issuing a Termination Notice Warning, and this was discussed. Cheron and the board were prepared to fight it when it came.

And it came.

But it had been a complete shock when the establishment announced that the school had seriously breached its financial regulations and hence they would be issuing the school with a Regulator's Sanction as well. Both notices would be published for the whole world to see. There had been no known irregularities at the school so this came without warning and without context. The team were visibly shocked as they faced yet another crisis. It was clear that the establishment were after Cheron.

# Chapter Seventeen – Crisis

Crises come in various forms. Local. National. Global.

The school was about to face all three.

## It Must Come Down

Back in the emergency meeting, Emilyn, the lead officer dealing with King Solomon's case in the establishment, explained the reasons for the Regulatory Sanction. This included a serious irregularity allegedly caused by Cheron. Thankfully, Carol Brown was completely aware of the item being raised and was able to challenge Emilyn. She agreed to go back and investigate further. But did she?

The meeting ended with an understanding that fifteen days' notice was to be given to the school with effect from the meeting, before either or both a Regulator's Sanction and the Termination Notice Warning were issued.

Sure enough, as expected, the Termination Notice Warning duly arrived. But not the Regulator's Sanction. The school was relieved. This had not been correct in the first place and an assumption was made that all was well, and having checked their facts, the establishment had withdrawn their threat.

Three weeks later all that changed. Cheron was still convalescing after her surgery when the email arrived. A Regulator's Sanction had been issued after all. Thirteen pages of it. Thirteen pages of false allegations and accusations. When Cheron read the sanction her initial reaction was that they had mistakenly sent it to the wrong school. The allegations were unrecognisable.

Two weeks before this, a local church minster, Joyce Fletcher, had been woken in the night with a sense that the school and Cheron in

# HR

Crisis

Crisis

particular were being targeted by antagonists and that she needed to specifically pray for Cheron.

Joyce found four photographs of Cheron online and printed them out. She then placed various scriptures from Psalm 56 over each photograph and began to pray blessing, success and protection over Cheron:

*Be gracious to me, O God, for man tramples on me; all day long an attacker oppresses me; my enemies trample on me all day long, for many attack me proudly. When I am afraid, I put my trust in you. In God, whose word I praise, in God I trust; I shall not be afraid. What can flesh do to me? . . . You have kept count of my tossings; put my tears in your bottle. Are they not in your book? Then my enemies will turn back in the day when I call. This I know, that God is for me . . . For you have delivered my soul from death, yes, my feet from falling, that I may walk before God.*

Joyce sent the Bible verses on to Cheron, explaining what she felt God had said. One of the comments from Joyce was that there were allegations against Cheron personally but that these allegations would not stick. The false allegations published would be taken down. It will come down. It must come down.

At the time, Cheron was grateful for Joyce's prayers, but she didn't understand what those allegations might be or what Joyce was saying. And there was no real understanding as to what Joyce meant by 'it will come down, it must come down'. With the arrival of the Regulator's Sanction and the seemingly personal attack on her own integrity, Cheron was beginning to understand the significance of Joyce's prophetic message.

Worse was to come. Going back on their fifteen-day promise, the establishment published the report on their website just one day after sending the findings to Cheron.

Cheron was distraught.

The immediate impact of the Regulator's Sanction going public was the response from many of the school's supporters. A number of high-profile supporters who were prepared to lobby for King Solomon's funding agreement not to be terminated, went quiet. Such was the devastating effect.

However, speculation within the community began to arise when they noted that another Trust had been given approval to open a free school in Birmingham. The Trust visited King Solomon to look at the building. Strange! Was the establishment trying to close down King Solomon in order to give this Trust the King Solomon building?

Support from the board was immediate. One or two held reservations about challenging the establishment for fear that the school would be subject to victimisation. But the board was courageous and made the decision to proceed. The findings were simply wrong. They would challenge the report. They would also challenge the establishment's practice of publishing a report without the school being able to fact check it first.

## Another God Incident

The former Lord Mayor of Birmingham, Dr Cllr Yvonne Mosquito, had now become the Deputy Lord Mayor. She had always been supportive of King Solomon but she was amongst those who, upon hearing the allegations against Cheron and King Solomon in the Regulator's Sanction, expressed concern. Other influential individuals withdrew support immediately. In one of those God-instances that others might call co-incidences, Cheron's sister Audrey had an unexpected phone call from Yvonne. Yvonne didn't know that the Audrey she was talking to was Cheron's sister. When the connection was made, they started talking about King Solomon. Audrey presented Yvonne with the key facts. Yvonne felt convicted to help.

Yvonne had a wide network of professional contacts which included people with expert knowledge of public sector regulations. Lin Rowe was ideal for this. But Lin was heavily involved in other things, so it was not looking hopeful. However, Lin had heard of Cheron and the Black Boys Can projects, so she was prepared to meet her and hear what Cheron had to say. The day after being asked, Lin and Dr Yvonne were knocking on Cheron's door whilst she was convalescing. They had come to help.

Cheron called Carol Brown, her vice chair, on the off chance, to see if she was available to come over to the meeting with Yvonne and Lin. Carol came. It took the best part of a day, given the sheer number of direct and indirect allegations, to review and challenge each indictment. Lin was convinced without a shadow of a doubt that King Solomon had a case.

Lin was better than any lawyer they had dealt with in the past, and she didn't want a penny from the school. A sandwich and a cup of tea would suffice.

An urgent meeting was requested with the director from the establishment who issued the sanction. To his credit, he responded straight away, and the meeting was arranged in London.

Regarding travelling down to London for the meeting, Carol was going to have to attend as Cheron was not well enough.

The meeting with Lin and Yvonne ended with a light chat about this and that. Not that Cheron was on death's door, but they also talked about Lin's funeral business!

The next morning Cheron got a call. Carol's father had passed away suddenly. This was sad news for all.

With Cheron being poorly and Carol suffering a bereavement, neither the chair nor vice chair were able to attend the meeting in London. Cheron made the decision she was going to go. She had to fight for the school. Carol also insisted that she was going too. She too had to fight. Both went with a determination to see justice done. Accompanying them were Lin and the executive heads.

After the pleasantries, the director invited Cheron to lead the rest of the meeting. Cheron presented each of the facts, making use of her colleagues as and when required. No one would have known how poorly Cheron was or that Carol was suffering from the sudden loss of her father just days before.

Lin was on form. She was highly experienced at dealing with regulatory matters. No one could pull the wool over her eyes. At one point in time the director tried to keep her quiet, but she made it clear why she was there. She had come to fight for King Solomon, to fight for justice.

The meeting ended after an hour, and by that time the two most serious allegations, including the one against Cheron personally, had been successfully refuted. Emilyn, the senior officer in charge of the case, confessed that she had not fact checked the accuracy of the allegations against Cheron nor King Solomon before publishing the sanction. Emilyn looked embarrassed. The regional manager looked embarrassed. The national director looked extremely embarrassed.

Senior government officials had relied on Emilyn's work and she had let them down badly. Would she be sacked? Rather timidly, Emilyn, with a quiet voice, asked Cheron if she was still prepared to work with her and her team. Cheron felt sorry for her. She accepted the offer.

The director agreed to take down the sanction temporarily and to investigate the remaining allegations against King Solomon. None of the officers present knew what the process was for taking down a sanction as the establishment had never had to do that before. King Solomon was a first. They had made history.

## It Came Down

The director was true to his word. In less than 24 hours the Regulator's Sanction was taken down. Taken down. 'It will come down; it must come down.' Just as Joyce Fletcher had prophesied, weeks before the sanction.

In her capacity of a regulatory officer, Emilyn attended the school several days later to investigate the remaining allegations. She brought a colleague with her.

There was clear uneasiness from Emilyn and her colleague but Cheron, Carol and Lin gave them the same degree of hospitality as they would to friends of the school. After they had completed their investigation, Cheron offered them lunch. They were taken aback by the offer; they were hungry, so gratefully accepted. They had lunch together and then requested a tour of the school. Emilyn and her colleague thanked them on their way out.

It was then that Emilyn confessed that she had been dreading the visit to the school; so much so that her stomach had been in knots during her train journey. They were grateful for the hospitality they had received. But there were no grudges. The school just wanted justice.

Emilyn promised to get back to Cheron in a matter of days with the outcome of the investigation.

But then the pandemic . . .

**Kindness**
**A King Solomon Value, the King Solomon Way**

Whatever happened to being kind
When did all think anger and cruel thoughts take over your mind

Take no notice of the voice inside your head telling you to be rude
But listen to the voice encouraging you to be . . .

Kindness is expressed in its generosity to others
Kind words, kind deeds as if they are a close friend, a sister or brother

Kindness combats rudeness and injustice
And aggressively overthrows cruelty and harshness

You may be thinking, that this is just a load of waffle
But this so-called waffle can unlock a new outlook in life and get others out of trouble

So be intentional about being kind, please don't delay
Make a difference to someone's life today

**Marcia – Year 11 Student, King Solomon International Business School**

## Worldwide Crisis

Huw Edwards had a particularly serious look on his face as he presented the BBC ten o'clock news. There were stories coming out of China of a new virus which was spreading rapidly. As Cheron watched the news that night, there was little consideration of a potential effect on the UK and the news concentrated on British nationals trying to get home as the pandemic began to spread.

By the end of that month, January 2020, there were two cases of Covid-19 in the UK. By 26th March, the whole country was in lockdown. No school. And for the first cohort of students – the children of the parents who had supported King Solomon from the beginning – no exams. No graduation. No end of year prom. All cancelled.

Cheron's letter to parents was heartfelt. There was a special letter for the Year 11 students meant to be completing their GCSE exams. The school would do all they could. They would help students with home studies. But this was a worldwide pandemic and it was not clear how long restrictions would last.

UNESCO reported 1.6 billion children were out of school around the world. Remote learning was the new phrase. This quickly highlighted the disparity between different schools in the UK. King Solomon has a disproportionate number of children eligible for free school meals. It's not the best of measures, but it highlights needs and reflective of that, the number of families without a computer, with no laptop, no wireless connection, no way of accessing remote learning.

Suddenly, the most important member of staff became the IT manager and as a result he and his team were working all the hours available. The Titan Partnership, a schools umbrella organisation, donated 20 laptops and this, along with an awareness as to how King Solomon was affected, led to the school being featured on the BBC news. Even when a laptop could be sourced, parents were often unprepared, some unable to manage the child in a home setting.

Add to that a disproportionate impact from the virus on black and Asian communities in the early days of lockdown and King Solomon was facing a significant challenge. A good number of staff were also from these communities, and many were off sick as a result. Some children lost members of their family as Covid-19 had its effect. The school also lost four key supporters to Covid during this time.

The school's faith principles served it well and this was a lifeline to many of the children, parents and staff. The global crisis was not going to stop the chaplaincy work. This was needed more than ever. Online assembles took place. Chaplains kept in touch with the children. Children fed back to the chaplains. They asked for prayer, they received prayer. Children, parents and staff reported losses. Chaplains prayed through every loss.

The school remained open for the children of frontline workers and for those who were vulnerable in a home setting. On the morning that two girls were due to meet Cheron for a commendation for developing an innovative business venture, only one girl arrived. The other had been rushed back home where a close member of their family was dying because of Covid. Such was the effect of Covid on the King Solomon community that hardly a child was unaware of someone who had died or who was fighting for their life in hospital.

Staff members also suffered loss. King Solomon gives permission to their family to express their faith and pastoring needs and to ask for help both inside and outside the school setting.

For some staff, King Solomon is the closest association they have to church, to faith. So, when the father of one of those staff died, she asked Pastor Doreen to oversee the internment of her father's ashes. The chaplaincy was introduced to her children, grandchildren and extended family. As they interred the ashes, the chaplaincy didn't do anything differently. They didn't have to put on a different form, a different hat, pretend to be anything else other than what they were in the school. They seamlessly transferred what they did at King Solomon to an external event, yet still representing the school. The family were grateful.

Mental health support for several students was required. The Grace Inclusion Centre experienced many more emotional issues than normal. Some of this sadly related to both family breakdown and loss, which increased during the lockdown. One of the positive effects relates to students appreciating school in a new way – when it wasn't there, they realised how much they missed it. Upon return to school, students were more amenable to study. There was more compassion. Students were more supportive towards each other.

During lockdown, it was reported that many people in the UK, and indeed throughout the world, suffered anxiety and depression. But parents reported how resourceful their children had become due to their learning at King Solomon. Children, even those from unchurched backgrounds, were reported to have read psalms to their family, prayed with them, encouraged them, sung songs they had learnt in assembly.

Even in a Covid crisis, there were positive moments.

## A Bag of Love

Schools throughout the country were locked down. Only children of frontline workers and vulnerable children were allowed to attend school for months. During this time, two of King Solomon's eight-year-old budding entrepreneurs, Kyomi Ferguson and Aryana Gooden, launched a new business. Called 'A Bag of Love', they purchased purple bags in line with the school colour and then filled them with a carefully selected range of items:

- A heart-shaped balloon to declare that love was in the air
- A packet of Love Hearts to show that there is a world of love
- A packet of hot chocolate for relaxing during those cold days
- A packet of tissues to wipe away any tears
- Some star bubbles to remind everyone that they are stars
- A Dove soap to remind them that they are beautiful
- A candle to lighten up the day
- A ladybird chocolate to remind them that spring is coming, there is hope

- A cross to remind them that Jesus died for their sins
- A prayer to bless them with Jesus' love
- A scripture quote from 2 Corinthians in the Bible to remind them to fix their eyes on what is unseen, not on what can be seen in front of them

The sales of the bags at £5 each were phenomenal. People were buying in bulk. Many of the lonely and forgotten during the Covid crisis received a Bag of Love by way of encouragement.

## The Book

For several years many people who had witnessed King Solomon and the constant challenges which the school victoriously overcame, had encouraged Cheron to write a book. Each time, year after year, her response had been consistent. 'No.'

Cheron lived life in the fast line and had no time to write. Each time the school came through another crisis, those dreaded words rolled off people's lips: 'You've got to write the book.' Members. Directors. Staff. Politicians. Friends. None of them got the positive response they were hoping for.

Then in March 2020 the pandemic hit. Everything shut down. Offices were closed. Schools were closed. Suddenly Cheron found herself out of the fast lane and onto the hard shoulder. It felt surreal. Now she had time on her hands; well at least for the first few weeks of lockdown. But it was during those first few weeks that the voices she heard over the years merged into one loud voice: 'You've got to write the book!'

David Illingworth was amongst those who kept urging Cheron to write. David is a Trust member. He has been a spiritual tower of strength for Cheron for many years. David and Audrey were like a spiritual tag team. One would get a vision and share it with Cheron, and shortly afterward the other would get the same vision. On one occasion, for example, they both saw a vision of God parting the Red Sea for King Solomon to walk through. On another occasion they both saw a vision of a crowd of angels supporting King Solomon.

A couple of years prior to this David informed Cheron that if she decided to write the book, he knew of a publisher that would be interested in her story. But was that lead still there? Cheron made a note in her 'to do list' for the following morning, to ring David and find out if he still had the contact with the publisher.

She rang him first thing the next morning. But before Cheron could say anything, David spoke first.

'Cheron, I've just come back from a prayer meeting. I was telling the group about King Solomon. You've got to write that book, Cheron.'

'Actually, David, that's precisely why I've called you, to let you know I've decided to write.'

'About time, Cheron!'

'David, are you still by any chance in touch with the publisher you mentioned to me a couple of years ago?'

'Well, you won't believe this, but I've got a meeting with him tomorrow morning at 10am. I'll try and broker this for you, Cheron. Leave it with me.'

David rang back the following day with the good news. The publisher was sold on the story.

'Fantastic, thanks David. The only problem is that I could do with someone to co-author it with me.'

'Leave it with me, Cheron. The publisher works with a lot of writers who I'm sure will be interested in your story.'

And this was how Cheron was introduced to Ralph Turner. How perfect. A Christian. A pastor. A former secondary school governor. A former chair of governors. This was the same Ralph Turner who had written loads of brilliant Christian books including the highly acclaimed biography of Gerald Coates and *Faith Man*, David Lamb's story. Cheron couldn't have asked for anyone better.

Cheron gave a brief outline of her story.

'Wow!' said Ralph. 'This is a story that needs to be told. It's compelling.'

'Ralph, I need to be open and honest with you at the outset. Things at the school are dire. We are at rock bottom. Ofsted rated our Early Years as good, and our primary school was also rated good, but because secondary was rated inadequate, then the school was deemed to be inadequate and placed in Special Measures. We are at risk of closure.'

'Oh dear,' said Ralph.

This was the last thing any author wanted to hear. This wasn't a success story; it was an utter and total disaster. The school was deep in the valley of the shadow of death.

There was silence on the line.

Cheron waited to hear what Ralph was going to say, expecting him to put the phone down, making a sharp exit from the project. But instead, he offered to pray.

Ralph prayed, rolled up his sleeves, picked up a pen and with a high degree of enthusiasm in his voice said, 'Now, let's get on with writing this book.'

Cheron couldn't believe what had happened. In just a matter of days she had decided to write the book, found the perfect co-author, and was signing a contract with a publisher.

In the middle of a schools' crisis, a national and global crisis, God had opened the door for the book to be written. Cheron walked through the open doors.

## Black Lives Matter

May 25th 2020. The day two young American girls had the courage to film his death. Kaylynn Gilbert, aged 17, and Alyssa Funari, aged 18, saw what was happening. Despite the threat of mace spray from the murderer, they kept filming as George Floyd died in front of their phone camera.

Their bravery means that the world is changing. Black Lives Matter. They always have. But that day in Minneapolis showed that they didn't seem to matter that much and that something needed to be done.

The response around the world was immediate. Black men have died before at the hands of the police, but usually it's in a far-off grainy image. The fact that this was a few feet away in front of a phone camera changed everything. This couldn't be hidden. In the 21st century, racial prejudice was alive and well.

The effect on King Solomon was immediate and dramatic. The school is predominantly black and Asian and the scenes on the news hit home. A deep, built-up grief surfaced for so many. This was different. This had to be different.

Despite Covid, many marched. Cheron joined them. Noticing her two nieces were part of a Solihull march, inspired her even more to join in. As with most of the marches, it was both peaceful and well organised. And one of the leaders turned out to be Anton Foster, now a millennial business owner and investor who, as a child, attended the launch of the very first Black Boys Can project.

The march highlighted the solidarity between blacks, Asian and whites. There was such a good mix. Cheron recognised others, of all colours, from her church in Solihull. And, of course, the black churches were particularly well represented. At one point, some of the young people on the march stopped to debate with some strong looking men who were acting as bodyguards for statutes in Solihull. They were not going to let those marching pull down their prized statutes. By the end of the debate, when they realised that the protestors were good law-abiding citizens who were simply protesting against racism and police brutality, and had no intentions of vandalising the statutes, some of the antagonists decided to join in the march declaring Black Lives Matter. Cheron was so proud of Anton.

## Head On

Back at the school Mrs Abrahams, assisted by Ms Allen, addressed the issues head on. They ensured an increased prominence for black history, especially regarding teaching on the two world wars. The Institute of Jamaica was invited to the school to present black history during lessons. Mrs Abrahams set up a special notice board to show the story of black Britain. A local artist contributed a picture of black students studying science. Each subject was reviewed to ensure there was a suitable cultural reflection within it.

Starting with training at an inset day, Ms Allen and the leadership team carried out a programme of discussion and debate throughout the school. Teachers spoke of their own stories, how they dealt with racism and how they overcame prejudice. Some of the most moving results from these discussions were several poems and prose pieces from the students where they were able to express their feelings and emotions in a constructive way.

There has been a noticeable increase in self-confidence among black students due to this initiative and this has shown itself in many ways, including a return to more natural hair styles.

Less constructive was the report of the Commission on Race and Ethnic Disparities on behalf of the government. Commonly known as the Sewell Report, this has caused a lot of concern. As one black Trust put it, the report's 'denial of the significance of structural racial and ethnic inequalities is particularly unsettling'. It is questionable as to whether the government at the time of this report had really understood the extent of the grief, anger and unrest among black communities. And to accept the findings of the report that racial inequalities are not an issue of deep concern in UK society is both sad and extremely short-sighted.

Add to that the views of a Home Secretary who considers that taking the knee at football games is 'gesture politics' and the gap between what is considered acceptable behaviour by the government and what is seen as acceptable among black communities, is vast.

Other responses have been more welcome. The shock of George Floyd's death in front of a camera has caused several black celebrities to speak out and subsequently for programmes to be made reflecting on their own struggles. Churches, charities and businesses have reviewed their policies, adding specific steps to ensure racial equality. All this is good news.

But it's only a beginning.

'We're not going back to where we were,' says Cheron. 'We have a long way to go but God is on the side of justice. I believe God is the one who will have the final say in this.'

### Black Lives Really Do Matter – Spoken Word

I will never understand the pain,
the fear of someone whose life could just be taken away,
because of their skin
or where they were born,
this world is a racist society where, it seems, people of colour
just don't matter.

I am white so I can walk down the street and turn a blind eye,
I can live my life like everything is fine,
I can ignore the cries and calls for justice
of innocent black lives taken because of prejudice.
I can easily forget that any of this is happening,
I can easily ignore the protests and fighting,
the fighting for rights for people of colour, the fighting for equality
in our society.
If justice wasn't served would it even matter to me?
If rights weren't gained would it affect me?
If nothing changed would I be bothered?
And yet I have a responsibility
As we are all part of one humanity.

George Floyd did not deserve to die.
George Floyd shouldn't have had to cry.
He should have been able to continue his life,
he should have arrived home safely that night.
Because of prejudice and discrimination
people like him are taken.
It is the twenty-first century
why is the world still fighting for equality?
I will never understand the pain,
but I will always stand with you until the day
that justice is served, and rights are gained
and people of colour no longer have to live afraid!

**Hanna Moore – Year 10 Student, King Solomon International
Business School**

## The Annual Praise Service

How can you possibly have an annual praise service in the middle of a crisis? Crisis in the school, crisis in the nation and crisis globally. That was the challenge for the leadership team. But the school had developed a culture of praise to God that was independent of whether things were going well or not. So the praise service went ahead as usual. Maybe not as normal as, due to Covid, it had to be held online.

Pastor Doreen led the way. Pre-recorded segments were arranged, including Cheron's message. Cheron was heartened to see the Christian values of the school reflected throughout. The rolling photo presentations included not just the children and their teachers but also the kitchen staff, caretakers, cleaners and so forth. Everyone was important. Everyone valued.

One of the songs that Cheron reviewed before the service went live was one that had been prepared by the primary school staff. They were all on there – the head, deputy head, the teachers and support staff. All on Zoom and all segued together into the full piece. And the piece itself? Gloria Gaynor's iconic song 'I Will Survive'.

A strange song for an annual praise service. Cheron did not think it was appropriate at first, but the more she watched it, the more she enjoyed it. Lots of fun being had by the staff and a fun song to sing. But in the midst of the song Cheron felt that God was speaking through it. That it was a prophetic declaration. The school would survive! If they knew 'how to love' they would survive. They would get through the crises surrounding them and they would see God bring them through.

The whole online praise event was a great success, not least the song.

A day later and Cheron was catching up with the deputy head of primary, Michelle.

'Cheron, I can't believe they included the primary staff singing Gloria Gaynor's secular song "I will Survive" in the praise service. I was so embarrassed.'

'What do you mean, Michelle?'

'It wasn't meant for the praise service. We only did it for ourselves for a laugh. It was never intended for public consumption! We weren't even trying! You can see it in the video – some of us are drinking mugs of tea, most of us laughing. Some of us are just miming and acting out the words. It was meant as a bit of fun for the primary staff, not for the praise service! The board saw it! The parents saw it! How embarrassing!'

'Michelle, it wasn't embarrassing at all. It was brilliant. The board loved it. The song was fun. But most of all it was God's encouragement to us. We *will* survive!'

## Influencing National Policy

Cheron had to leave the praise service early, along with the executive heads. They were due to take a Zoom meeting with the regulators and hear the outcome of their investigation into the original 13-page report.

As they left the praise service to join the regulators' Zoom meeting, there was a praise song sounding out. Reuben and Micah were singing. Both boys had by now found a faith in Christ which resulted in a complete turnaround. They were singing 'I Am Not Alone', a song based on the famous Psalm 23, the Lord is my shepherd. There was one particular verse of that psalm that rang out in Cheron's mind as she went to join the Zoom meeting. 'Even though I walk through the darkest valley, I will fear no evil, for you are with me; He always guides me through mountains and valleys.' The words seemed so appropriate for the crises they had been through locally, nationally and globally.

Cheron was confident in what she was about to hear on the next Zoom call. And she wasn't disappointed.

Emilyn, the lead officer, explained that the Regulator's Sanction that had been published and then temporarily taken down would not be going back up. Instead, King Solomon would be issued with a formal apology. In addition, they were going to change their national policy to ensure that all academy trusts in the country are given the opportunity to fact check draft documents before they are published.

Cheron sat back in her chair, a silent prayer ascending to the heavens. To the God who was greater than Covid. To the God of justice for black lives. To the God who had seen the school through valleys and shadows.

*Even though I walk through the valley of the shadow of death, I will fear no evil, for you are with me.*

# Chapter Eighteen – The Favour Of God

With the global pandemic, the matriculation ceremony at the beginning of the new school year in September 2020 needed to be different. The school arranged for three separate ceremonies to maintain Covid compliance. The new Sixth Form students from the Sturridge Football Academy felt particularly welcomed. There was a great synergy between the school and the Academy.

## Parental choice

Amongst those being matriculated in the primary and secondary schools were the children of Bret Jim. Bret, a senior educational leader in a college, is a practising Christian. He and his wife, both highly educated professional parents, chose King Solomon for their children despite the challenges the school was facing. But why?

**Parental Choice . . . Why We Chose to Send Our Children to King Solomon**

My wife and I chose to send our children to King Solomon because it's a Christian's school. Because of the vision. Because it's unique. Because the school is centred on Christ. It is very unusual to see such a school in an age where Christianity is being marginalised.

We are both highly educated so the education of our children is important to us, but so is their spiritual development. We were looking for a Christian school which was not just Christian in name only.

We undertook our due diligence on the school and we were fully aware that King Solomon had challenges. We read the Ofsted reports, we read the Termination Warning letter.

We visited the school open day and looked beyond the usual, often superficial, marketing spiel that schools make to attract parents to their school. We loved what we heard and saw. We saw, as we came down the stairs, a child who was very distressed and one of the staff offering to pray for the child. It was just great to see. This is a school where there is freedom to pray, a place where a child who is having a bad day can get spiritual support. In most schools that would be frowned upon, but not at King Solomon.

What school doesn't have any form of challenge? King Solomon is a new school. Starting anything new often comes with challenges. We didn't want to stand on the outside and criticise it or wait for the school to overcome its challenges. No, we wanted to be part of the journey to it becoming outstanding, so we chose King Solomon.

When the opportunity came for me to stand for election to become a Parent Governor, I took it. I was elected. I deem it a privilege to serve in this capacity and am totally committed to doing everything within my knowledge and ability to propel and further develop the exciting vision of this school.

**Bret Jim – Elected Parent Governor**

## The Commissioner's Meeting

Although the Regulator's Sanction had been rescinded, the Termination Notice Warning remained. Another battle to face.

Before the pandemic, Cheron had requested a meeting with Andrew Warren, the Regional Schools Commissioner for the West Midlands. King Solomon needed to put up a good fight if it was to survive.

The meeting couldn't take place for months because of the national pandemic. But a date was finally agreed for November 2020.

Clive kept reminding Cheron, 'It's not over till it's over.' David Illingworth encouraged her that God will make a way for King Solomon, but also reminded her that God didn't remove the Red Sea when Pharaoh was after the children of Israel, he parted it.

The meeting, when it happened, was held online. A verbal presentation from Cheron, Carol, Mrs Abrahams and Mrs Popratnjak was supported by Chris Wright, from Woodard Schools. It was significant evidence of their commitment to give a vote of confidence to the school that despite all the challenges King Solomon had faced, Woodard wished to continue their relationship.

Despite some compelling arguments, it appeared to Cheron that the Commissioner had already made his mind up before hearing their presentation about the future of King Solomon as in his closing remarks he said he was contemplating which multi-academy trust would be best to take over the running of King Solomon. After the meeting Cheron reminded the Commissioner that while he had the power to terminate King Solomon's funding agreement, it was a power rather than a duty, and therefore he didn't have to. He could instead decide to support the school.

Cheron and the team waited for the outcome of the meeting against a backdrop of the Black Lives Matter concerns. The BBC had been showing a number of Steve McQueen's *Small Axe* drama series, highlighting how badly blacks had been treated in the UK over the years. It included the film *Mangrove*, a true story of the Mangrove restaurant, a lively community hub in London's Notting Hill that was the subject of relentless racist police raids during the 1970s, and a consequent trial. As far as the antagonists were concerned, black people shouldn't own their own businesses. They should be kept in their 'place'. It felt as if King Solomon had suffered that same prejudice. It was not their 'place' to own a school. The number of investigations. The unfair accusations. The additional hoops that they had needed to jump through. The simple fact that throughout all the processes it had consistently been white people deciding the fate of black people. Surely it was time for change? Surely it was time to support King Solomon, not condemn it?

Once again Cheron's prayer partners were praying before her remote meeting with the Commissioner.


## Crunch Time

Cheron braced herself. This was the crunch moment.

She remembered the Commissioner saying at the meeting in November that he was considering which would be the best multi-academy trust to take over King Solomon. Was he still on that page?

What would the decision be? Questions flooded her mind.

Did the Commissioner understand the vision for King Solomon and what the school was trying to achieve? Has the Commissioner taken account of the unique set of adverse circumstances the school has faced including factors which were completely out of their control? Did he recognise that all-through schools are the most complex type of schools to run? Had he taken account of the fact that the school was in one of the most deprived economic and social wards in the country? Had he really listened to the team's strong defence? Did he recognise the unique contribution King Solomon brings to the educational landscape of Birmingham, to the West Midlands, to the country? Was the Commissioner anti blacks or a white ally? Was he pro or anti faith schools? Did he know about the widely held view that the black majority led schools in Birmingham had not been given a fair chance to succeed?

Did the Commissioner . . .? Was the Commissioner . . .? Would the Commissioner . . .? The questions overflowed.

Then Andrew Warren, the Commissioner, summed up the factors he had taken into account. He acknowledged that King Solomon is a complex school and that its vision was compelling.

That word again. Compelling.

Then he gave his verdict. He was prepared to give the school more time to turn around.

Another chance! That's all she needed! He had listened.

He went on to inform Cheron that he was prepared to set up a new innovative school improvement project to support King Solomon. This would be the first project of its kind in the country. It would involve a package of support to enable the school to propel its vision and bring about rapid and sustained improvement. The package of support would include the appointment of new directors to the existing board, and a school improvement partner with an excellent track record. There were several non-negotiable conditions attached to his decision. They would have to agree to it.

Baroness Berridge, the academies minister, gave her full backing to this innovative project as she had already bought into King Solomon's vision. Other government ministers were also supportive of the project. The project was approved by Gavin Williamson, the Secretary of State.

The Trust members and the board of directors at King Solomon agreed to the conditions attached to the project. There was a sense of both relief and celebration. The school had come through a real storm. The valleys had been deep, and the shadows had been dark. But here was a lifeline, a Commissioner who saw the school's potential and was offering the school what he considered to be a genuine way to fulfil their ambitions.

## Television

Celebrations continued throughout that Christmas period and beyond.

Within a short space of time there were several TV appearances from King Solomon students, staff and supporters.

The school featured on BBC *Midlands Today* news, highlighting the impact of Covid on disadvantaged students. Later the school featured again on the news, with a celebration of black hair.

The school's careers advisor, Kameese Davis, entered BBC 1's *Dragons' Den* and struck a deal for a £50,000 investment with a Dragon, Sara Davis. What a motivating factor for the budding entrepreneurs at King Solomon!

Stephen Brooks featured on the No 10 Downing Street's daily Covid-19 briefing, posing a challenging question to the Prime Minster.

Then Dionne Rey, a middle leader at King Solomon, appeared in the audience on Ant and Dec's *Saturday Night Takeaway*, and was selected to win a prize.

Wesley and Jordan Henry, alumni of Excell3's Black Boys Can project, were on *The Voice* UK. They got through to the highly competitive semi-final.

The BBC 1 Christmas *Songs of Praise* came from the Church of God of Prophecy. And it is worth remembering that they are Pentecostals, and that Pentecostals had been condemned by the education authorities as being a cult those years previously. Now a Pentecostal church is on primetime television hosting the morning service on Christmas Day. As Cheron watched the service, she saw many recognisable faces. The soloist was Joanne Hurlock, the former employee of Excell3 who had led the worship at the school's very first matriculation service in 2015. In the worship band were friends and relatives linked to the school. The brother of Esron, Excell3's graphic designer who designed King Solomon's logo, was on the drums. The son of Joyce Fletcher, one of King Solomon's key prayer supporters, was on the bass guitar. Annette B, Cheron's younger sister, was among the singers. And the icing on the cake was seeing Imaani Davis, aged 9, a King Solomon primary student, reading the Christmas scripture to the nation.

Such a wonderful moment of praise and thanksgiving.

## The Project Begins

Cheron was looking forward to the commencement of the new innovative school improvement project. There were great hopes that the standards in the secondary school would catch up with and become as good as the Early Years and primary school. The new highly experienced directors were to join the board and work alongside the existing directors. A new school improvement partner was appointed to bring about rapid and sustained improvement. This was an innovative project, the first of its kind in the country. King Solomon, a black majority led school, was to be the first beneficiary of this initiative. But how would the King Solomon antagonists within the establishment respond to this? Would they resent King Solomon being afforded this opportunity? Time would tell.

The project was now ready to commence. The Commissioner called Cheron and Mrs Abrahams to a meeting to introduce them to the key project members.

The Commissioner had initiated the project but were all the project members committed to its success?

Alarm bells rang when Cheron realised that one of the school's known antagonists in the establishment was to be involved in the project. Let's call him Pharaoh, as he was as much of an antagonist of King Solomon as the renowned Pharaoh of the Old Testament was antagonistic towards the children of Israel, wanting to keep them in bondage. Even after he let them go, he aggressively pursued them. This Pharaoh represents all of King Solomon's antagonists rolled into one, including those with a vendetta against Cheron and the team for being the only Trust in the country to have challenged and succeeded in getting the regulators sanction issued against them rescinded.

Further alarm bells rang when Cheron and Mrs Abrahams were informed that eight additional directors had been selected by the establishment to join the board. This meant that these eight directors would be able to outvote the existing seven directors if they so wished. In recruiting them, had the establishment paid attention to their 'fit' to King Solomon, to its vision, values and school demographics? Or was there something else in play?

The new school improvement partner was appointed by and accountable to the establishment, not to the King Solomon board. Were they the right school improvement partner for King Solomon? Would they really work in partnership with the senior leaders and the school? Would they propel the Christian ethos and the vision forward?

Something wasn't right, and Cheron knew it. This no longer felt like a partnership of equals but more like a hostile takeover. Cheron felt constrained to say something about this at the introductory meeting. Using metaphorical language, she said:

'I knew this was going to be an arranged marriage but I was expecting King Solomon's marriage partner to have four limbs. But now I've arrived at the alter I'm surprised to find that our partner has eight limbs. But we'll make it work.'

There was deadly silence for a few seconds. They knew what she was implying. Some did not react, one or two smiled, and others looked at her with stern faces and ice-cold eyes.

King Solomon's antagonists were now not only in the establishment but in the school as well. The project was about to begin, but the project members were not united. On the one side were those who wanted the project to work, and on the other side was Pharaoh and his minions whose mission appeared to be to tear down this black majority led Christian school.

## El Roi, the God Who Sees Me

An impressive array of directors were now on the board. Amongst them were chairs of multi-academy trusts, CEOs of multi-academy trusts, a governance lawyer, as well as headteachers and principals. Others came with additional expertise in areas such as pupil premium and special educational needs and disability. These eight directors had been recruited, some 'very carefully recruited', from all over the country. Quite naturally, onlookers had great expectation of these directors. How many boards could boast such an array of expertise, not to mention the expertise that was already present before they joined?

Cheron was determined to do everything she could to make the project work. Her top priority, as chair of the board, was to make sure these new directors were in positions to enable them to utilise their expertise to drive school improvement, particularly in the secondary school. Cheron didn't wait until the start of the new academic year to make their appointments but called a board meeting the same week the new directors joined and nominated them to sit on and lead committees as well as serving as link directors. All of her nominations were accepted. They were all set to go.

The school improvement partner's team also started work straight away. Amongst them was a lead Ofsted inspector. Unlike typical school improvements partners who visit a school every half term, this partner was going to work full-time in the school. They requested an office and moved into the school.

Some of the new directors genuinely wanted King Solomon to succeed. Some, such as Alan and Max, offered sound advice. Others, such as Christopher and Nigel, supported and constructively challenged the school leadership. However, with the infiltration of Pharaoh's minions Cheron felt that the long-established culture of respect, trust and mutual cooperation had been replaced by an atmosphere of distrust, disrespect, obstruction and aggression.

Two years before the project began, a pastor's wife shared with Cheron a word of knowledge which she felt she had received from God. Cheron was told that the board would become very aggressive, and some directors would be hostile towards her. Some time later, another Christian shared a similar message, but this time it was much worse, with the suggestion that the hostility would not just come from the boardroom. At the time, Cheron was baffled as there was a mutual respect between the board and in the school. She couldn't envisage anyone behaving like that. The messages were put to the back of her mind. But both of these messages proved to be prophetic. They were accurate. God is all knowing. Nothing and no one is hidden from Him. He is the God of the present. And He is the God of the future.

Pharaoh's minions sometimes treated Cheron as though she were invisible. She shared this at a meeting with the establishment. Later that afternoon, when she went back to work, her eyes were drawn to a video thumbnail on her computer screen. As she looked closely, she saw a picture of a black woman and was taken aback when she read the caption in bold, 'you are not invisible to God'. God's word for her, just at the moment she needed it.

## Another Sanballat Letter

The board of directors became increasingly toxic. One of Pharaoh's minions sent in another one of those Sanballat letters, anonymously, to the establishment. Another critical persecutor penning false allegations against King Solomon, which, if founded, could lead to action being taken against the school. But like all the previous allegations, these were unfounded. The school was once again exonerated. This was great news, but it was wearing. The school was constantly being distracted, having to devote time and energy defending allegation after allegation, rather than focusing on the vision and driving the school forward.

Shortly afterwards the minion boasted that he had written the Sanballat letter. But Cheron already knew that, so it wasn't news. But what was particularly interesting was discovering the identity of a member of staff with divided loyalty, who had become a Fifth Columnist for the minions. The staff member was leaking information and disinformation about operational matters to Pharaoh's minions and they leaked it to the establishment. Mrs Abrahams was totally unaware of this member of staff's actions. When the staff member decided to leave the school, Pharaoh's minions gave her an unusual amount of support.

The school leadership felt a continuing negative impact of Pharaoh and the minions. What had been a stable leadership team was now breaking up. Mrs Abrahams loved the school dearly but hated the politics associated with the project. She resigned. Even Stephen Brooks, who had been the bedrock of King Solomon and the glue that had helped to hold the school together over the years, made the difficult decision to resign.

In some areas the secondary school was making progress but in many respects the school was moving backwards. Ofsted was due to come out for another monitoring visit. Cheron and others predicted that the outcome would be negative. They were proved to be right.

When Cheron and key people within the Christian and black community became aware that the project was being derailed, they brought it to the attention of the establishment. Sadly, the establishment turned a blind eye and left Pharaoh and his minions unchecked. Details of what they did will not be shared in this book but suffice to say that within a matter of a few months, the project was completely derailed.

The Commissioner advised that King Solomon should consider joining a multi-academy trust, commonly referred to as a MAT. This was not what Cheron and those committed to the school wanted to hear. They had ambitions to establish their own MAT. Even senior officials in the establishment who recognised the unique contribution of King Solomon to the educational landscape believed that there was a need for more King Solomon type schools in the region. The overall project had been intended to advance the school to the point where King Solomon could pursue its dream of developing its own MAT, but that dream was being stifled.

## I Can't Breathe

Reluctantly, Cheron advised the board to set up a working party to explore MAT options. For Cheron and the old board of directors, exploring MAT options would include not just looking at existing MATs but also partnering with other similar schools to form a MAT. What Cheron didn't want was a continuation of the pattern of the black community being disenfranchised from the running of schools. Whatever Trust or schools they partnered with had to have shared Christian values where black Christians would be respected enough to be able to sit around the decision-making table at both member and board level as equals. After all, there would be no engagement period. Once it was part of a MAT, that would be it. Final.

But Cheron felt that Pharaoh and his minions were still suffocating King Solomon. The school was crying out, 'I can't breathe.'

King Solomon had to be saved somehow. Cheron put forward a proposal to the establishment. There was no response.

Much prayer went up for the school from various prayer groups. Everyone knew this was a fierce battle but all were trusting God. Acocks Green's House of Praise consistently prayed for King Solomon. Trust members Dr Adesola, Dr Lindsay and David Illingworth met regularly in the mornings for prayer before they began their busy day. There may have been discord at board level, but right at the top of the governance structure the Trust members stood united in prayer.

The school improvement partner, unexpectedly, announced that they were pulling out of the project. They claimed they couldn't build leadership capacity as the executive head and another senior leader had resigned. The remaining six senior leaders and five middle leaders continued to work hard.

Cheron and Carol and a number of other directors were then called to an urgent meeting with the Commissioner. Was the meeting to explore Cheron's proposal to get the project back on track? Was there another proposal? The Department for Education had plans to use the National Leader of Education headteachers to support standalone schools facing challenges. Would King Solomon be offered this? Cheron sensed it was going to be bad news. She was right. The Commissioner announced that the project had to end. He put forward his reasons as to why the project couldn't continue. He went on to strongly advise that the board should transfer King Solomon to a MAT. The establishment had already lined everything up for the takeover to commence. This was not what Cheron or Carol wanted to hear, but Cheron felt she should not be fighting this battle. She offered up no resistance. She remained at peace.

The song 'Still', sung by two of King Solomon's students had remained on her playlist during this season rang in her ears:

*Find rest my soul*
*In Christ alone*
*Know His power*

*In quietness and trust*
*When the oceans rise and thunders roar*
*I will soar with you above the storm*
*Father, You are King over the flood*
*I will be still, know You are God*

(Written by Reuben Morgan. © 2002 Reuben Morgan and Hillsong Publishing)

But most schools who voluntarily transfer to a MAT decide which MAT they join, subject to the Department for Education's approval. King Solomon was not going to be afforded the opportunity to choose. The establishment would make the decision. This was devastating news. The working party set up to explore MAT options had to be disbanded.

The establishment narrowed down their selection to two large MATs, both of which had over thirty schools, some of which were in Birmingham.

The Commissioner assured Cheron and the team that irrespective of which MAT King Solomon was transferred to, the Christian faith designation status under the Order of St Leonard, together with the vision, would be transferred with King Solomon. Cheron and Carol were grateful to the Commissioner for this.

Cheron, in her capacity of chairperson, in taking the Commissioner's advice, now had to lead the board in making a formal resolution to transfer King Solomon to a MAT. With grave reluctance, Cheron put forward the resolution that the board should voluntarily transfer King Solomon to a MAT. Pharaoh's minions were taken aback. They were expecting Cheron to resist the Commissioner's advice. The look of shock on some of their faces was a sight to behold. But it was a difficult decision for those who were committed to King Solomon and who wanted the school to remain in the hands of the black majority Christian community that set it up. For others, however, it was an easy decision. Some of them voted with great enthusiasm. Cheron, along with the entire board including all of the Christian Trust members and directors, were now going to have to leave the school and hand it over to another Trust.

With the decision having been made, Cheron metaphorically put King Solomon in a basket and sailed it down the river, not knowing where it would end up, but trusting God for its future.

## Staffing Pressures

Staff had to be informed that King Solomon was going to be taken over by a MAT. But they already had a lot to contend with. The school had faced considerable disruption due to staff and pupil absences caused by the pandemic. The whole of the school community had been especially hard-hit. Some had experienced bereavement. Some had been hospitalised with Covid. Some were suffering from long-term Covid and some were still self-isolating. The staff had been working exceptionally hard against the odds, supporting families and children affected whilst still trying to do their best for the school.

Now, in the midst of all that, the announcement of Mrs Abrahams' resignation was made. This came as a shock to many. Then on the same day staff were informed that Ofsted was coming in the following morning. The timing couldn't be worse. And this was then followed by yet another major announcement: King Solomon was to be taken over by a MAT. All of these announcements were made in a single day. It was an enormous amount for staff to take in. It was destabilising.

There were so many questions about the takeover. Where would King Solomon end up? Which large MAT was going to take them over? Would it be the right MAT for King Solomon? Are they a Christian

MAT? Did they have a good track record of delivering equal outcomes for their black students as well as their white counterparts? Did they have a black CEO? A Christian CEO? How many black headteachers, Christian headteachers did they have? More and more questions . . .

## An Orphan

Everyone waited to hear. The board waited. The staff waited. The parents waited. The community waited.

Once transferred to their MAT, that would be it. Another forced marriage, but this time a permanent one.

The suspense ended. The announcement was made. King Solomon would be transferred to Falcon Education Academies Trust.

Falcon? Everyone asked the same question. Who is Falcon? No one had heard of them. Falcon wasn't a big established MAT with over thirty schools. On the contrary, Falcon was a new secular MAT with two schools.

On 11th February 2022, the *TES Magazine* said the Department for Education had previously helped to launch the Falcon Education Trust to take on so-called 'orphan schools'. An orphan? King Solomon was in effect being transferred to an orphanage for schools. But King Solomon isn't an orphan. It had a Father, and its Father God certainly was not dead.

Falcon boasts of being an innovative project that supports schools to make rapid and sustainable improvements within 18 months. They then transferred them to a permanent MAT.

If Falcon were anything like the falcon bird, then they would have exceptional powers of vision, and have the ability to fly at high speed enabling King Solomon to become a good to outstanding school within 18- months. Would they live up to their name? Would they have the vision to see King Solomon's potential and purpose and propel it to fly at speed? Would they maintain the strong Christian ethos? Would they respect and effectively engage with King Solomon's stakeholders, including the black Christian community? Would they propel the vision of the school to encourage, nurture and support budding entrepreneurs? Would they give local black Christian stakeholders seats around the decision-making table in the boardroom? Now that King Solomon was to be in the hands of Falcon, would it at last be free from the relentless and aggressive pursuit of antagonists?

Cheron encouraged staff, parents and the community to work with the incoming MAT to drive the school forward and propel the vision. Mrs Kent, the head of primary, was to become a key player in this, being the most senior member of staff to transfer into the MAT. This was the second time Mrs Kent was required to become interim accounting officer, to be the anchor during troubled times. Once again, Mrs Kent stepped up to the mark, embraced the challenge and held the fort whilst the school went through the transition.

Interestingly, around the same time that the announcement was made that King Solomon would be transferred temporarily to Falcon, Cheron met for the first time, the father of a boy that her parents had been fostering. Upon meeting Cheron, the boy's father expressed his gratitude to Cheron's family for looking after his son. Despite the numerous disadvantages his son had faced, he capitalised on the opportunities afforded him from the Black Boys Can project and wider Excell3 programmes. His son now had a first-class honours degree and was undertaking a master's degree. His father was so proud of his son, and extremely grateful to Cheron's family for taking him into their home. Will Cheron and the team in the next year or two be able to look back and say to Falcon, 'Thank you for looking after King Solomon, we are proud of the school'? The expectation is that we will.

Reflections On The Fight

# Chapter Nineteen – On The Couch

A group of six students came into the room. All from King Solomon School, they were to form a panel to conduct reflective interviews with Dr Cheron Byfield, the founder, Revd David Carr from the Order of St Leonard, the school's faith authority, and Pastor Doreen Makaya, the school's lead chaplain.

The representatives from the primary school were Aaron Ajayi, a founding primary school student, and Mayah Mian, both in Year 6. Representing the secondary school was Reuben Johnson, a founding secondary school student, now an alumnus in Year 13 at a local college. Representing the Sixth Form were Dinari Francis-Henry, Joel Engo Mulumba, and Crosby Bakare, all of whom are training at the Sturridge Football Academy.

In front of the students was a large couch. All three interviewees sat together, coffee in hands, notebooks on laps.

'Well,' said Cheron, 'this will be fun! Please feel free to ask anything. Your questions will help inform the readers of the book. You will be asking questions on their behalf. It will help us too – when we're asked challenging questions, it helps us think through issues we may not have been able to articulate previously.'

## Vision

### Q: Aaron

I have a vision board. My vision board keeps me focused on the goals and dreams I have for the key stages of my life. Dr Byfield, you have developed a compelling vision for the school which many people have bought into, but do you have a vision board for King Solomon, and, if so, on reflection would you say the vision is on track?

## A: Dr Byfield

Wow, Aaron. You're only 10 years of age and you have a vision board. I'm impressed. Well done.

Yes, you are right, many people bought into the vision. The Department for Education bought into it. Parents bought into it. Staff bought into it. The community bought into it. Even the landlord whom we bought the school building from bought into it.

King Solomon has something similar to a vision board. It's a document we call a strategic plan.

I wish I could say that the school is fully on track in delivering on the vision but it's not. We have done very well in delivering on some aspects of our vision, but not all. Generally, the Early Years phase and the primary school are more or less on track, but the secondary school has been slower – but is making progress.

There are challenges in starting any new major project, but King Solomon has faced a number of rather unique challenges which were outside of our control. Nonetheless, with hindsight there are a number of things we could have done differently or better which would have propelled the vision at a faster pace. But we are getting there.

# Fruit of the Spirit

## Q: Mayah

Why is character development so important at King Solomon? Secondly, are there better virtues we could use to develop students' character rather than the nine virtues associated with the Fruit of the Spirit which we currently use?

## A: Dr Byfield

A great education is considered by many to be about achieving academic qualifications. However, I believe we need so much more than that. A great education should also involve developing the character of students as well. The world is full of people who are highly educated with lots of qualifications but who lack moral character. This country is considered to have one of the best education systems in the world, yet at every level of our society there are far too many people devoid of character.

At King Solomon we are witnessing students who have grown in character. Students who treat others the way they want to be treated, who stand against injustice and inequality, who get involved in social action initiatives, who treat others in the right way even when they don't treat them well, who are positive, peacemakers, polite, meek but not weak, reliable, trustworthy, and exercise self-control. Our prayer is that as our students' character is transformed, they in turn will transform others in their families, in their workplace, in their business, in the boardroom, in society.

## A: Revd David Carr

Yes, I agree with Dr Byfield, character is absolutely essential and, no, there isn't a better framework to develop students' character than the virtues associated with the Fruit of the Spirit. The Fruit of the Spirit personifies the character of Christ. It is both passive and aggressive.

Love could be seen as passive, yet it is aggressive because it overcomes hatred.

Joy replaces sorrow and weeping.

Peace neutralises friction.

Patience subdues frustration.

Kindness and goodness combat rudeness and abuse.

Faithfulness stands unmovable in the face of compromise.

Gentleness replaces harshness . . . and finally, self-control defeats out-of-control.

Jesus lived on earth for 33 years. He spent the first 30 years, i.e. 90 per cent of those years, manifesting exemplary character, the Fruit of the Spirit. Building on this, He ministered for three years applying the unique skills and abilities given by the Holy Spirit to serve God for the benefit of people. This is known as the Gift of the Spirit, or the charisma of Christ. The combination of 90 per cent character, and 10 per cent charisma, should be the example to us all. Children who commit their lives to Christ, who develop in the Fruit of the Spirit, will be positioned to manifest the Gift of the Spirit.

## Turbulence

### Q: Rueben

Pastor Doreen, you were introduced to King Solomon whilst experiencing extreme turbulence on an airplane. This school has witnessed constant turbulence over the years. How have you made sense of these turbulences?

### A: Pastor Doreen Makaya

I can best explain this with a story told by one of our church leaders: a pilot. While flying, he explained, he occasionally felt a sort of temporary delusion that he was upside-down; this happened most whenever the clouds impaired his view, making it difficult to tell whether he was above or below them. He had, however, learned at such times to keep his eyes on the aircraft's attitude indicator, which informs him whether he's upright or not. If nothing was untoward, he was trained to keep the wings of the craft straight and level, never altering his course; in other words – stick to the plan!

Our own journey through times of turbulence was very similar to the pilot's: times when challenges threatened to obscure the vision of the school, erode the confidence of staff and the wider school family, and obscure our focus in the struggles of the short term. Nevertheless, God gave me, and others, the reassurance that the school was always a 'God idea', and that was the reassurance I needed to trust Him for the outcome. This is the mind-set that the King Solomon family has held close to heart in these hard times.

Pilots almost assuredly learn how to navigate stormy weather from practice and experience as much as controlled-environment training, and I believe the same can be said for our school community. Rather than destroying our vision, turbulence has provided the key pressure for its refinement in the past years.

Riding out turbulence is an inevitable but invaluable experience. Many challenges – like teaching in portacabins, prolonged building refurbishments or the poor Ofsted report – can leave us distracted and overwhelmed but can also be critical opportunities to learn and change. We must exploit unscheduled chances like these to model the core virtues of the school and cultivate the Fruit of the Spirit.

The pilot who relayed this story learned how to change his perspective by not concentrating on the clouds or even the sensation of turbulence but by keeping his eyes on the attitude indicator. We've had to remain focused on the bigger picture of God's plan, and at times adjust our attitudes to maintain a godly attitude.

Turbulence served to draw us closer to God. We had to learn to listen for His guidance.

The lights in an aircraft can sometimes go out during turbulence. And as a passenger on board of King Solomon, things at times have appeared dark on our school journey, but God has been teaching us never to doubt in the darkness, but to stay focused on the vision with the understanding that He would perform it.

I have been reassured time and time again by the voice of the pilot, our heavenly Father. So in times of turbulence, don't be tempted to make drastic changes, 'be still' and allow the voice of the pilot, your heavenly Father, to reassure and guide you. As the pilot checks the 'attitude indicator', take the time to calmly assess the situation and see what you can learn.

## Injustice

### Q: Rueben

I was considered to be the most challenging student at King Solomon. I would have been excluded from the school had it not been for people like you, Dr Byfield, and Dr Trevor Adams, who chose instead to support me. It not only turned me around but along the way I decided to give my life to Christ. Today I am a practising Christian with a strong desire to do good in the world. But King Solomon itself has experienced exclusion. Excluded from the government academy sponsorship programme and now excluded from making a decision about the future of King Solomon. On reflection, what do you think students and alumni of King Solomon can learn from this?

### A: Dr Cheron Byfield

I am so proud of you and many of our students that have graduated from King Solomon. You are a credit to us.

It can be disheartening when I reflect on where we could have reached today after being on this academy journey for 14 years. Undoubtedly, we made some mistakes along the way, but then others did also, but that didn't hinder them from progressing. It's not been a level playing field. Many academy trusts started long after us but today they are large multi-academy trusts. It's an unjust world. And even when we were given a chance to get onto the level playing field, this was met with strong resentment by our antagonists.

Every community should have a fair and equal chance of having a place in every sector of society. But the reality is that they don't. Not in the housing sector. Not in the education sector.

But there is hope.

The global Black Lives Matters protests that took place following the brutal killing of George Floyd was a powerful reminder that there is still a hunger for justice in this world. A hunger from every race, colour and culture.

Always remember there is good and bad in every race, so don't ever fall into the trap of pigeon-holing people. No race, colour or culture is perfect. The younger generation in particular provides us with hope. Amongst them are our allies from every ethnicity including our white allies, as well as Christians and those of other faiths and no faith who marched side by side with the black community fighting for justice. Value them.

God loves justice; therefore all Christians should engage in the righteous struggle for racial justice. I am so pleased that Christians in the UK celebrate Racial Justice Sunday. The organisers of Racial Justice Sunday argue that 'Racism and racial discrimination are justice issues because they deny basic justice and human dignity.'

A word of advice! Guard your heart against embitterment and ensure forgiveness towards those who treat you unfairly in life. Don't treat them the way they treat you. Always remember that you are a King Solomon student or alumnus, so live out those character virtues associated with the Fruit of the Spirit which you have been taught.

I commend all Christian pioneers – whether they are still around or not – particularly those in the independent sector where it is increasingly challenging to finance schools without government support.

I commend all the black educational pioneers whether they are still around today or not. Pioneers of Saturday schools, free schools and independent schools, including other Birmingham schools such as Kajans, Harper Bell, Platinum, the CUL Academy and others. I salute them all.

## Lessons Learnt

### Q: Dinari, Joel and Crosby

In reflecting on the last seven years, have there been any lessons you have learnt?

### A: Dr Byfield

I wish I could say no, we did everything right, we never made any mistakes, but I can't.

If we were to start a new school again, one thing we would ensure is that we have the building ready. Operating a school from portacabins would not be an option I would even consider. The second thing is making sure we have the right principal for this school. We would definitely engage in headhunting for a principal rather than relying on traditional methods of recruitment. Headhunting has proven to be the best option for us.

One afternoon two board members, Clive Bailey and Carol Brown, met me for coffee. During that time, we embarked on a brutally honest reflection of our decision-making process for selecting principals over the years. We were very critical of ourselves. Following that meeting I began to search for biblical principles for making wise decisions. Out of that process emerged seven principles. Retrospectively I used those principles for assessing every single principal we had employed. It was a very revealing and worthwhile exercise. There were times we had clearly made the wrong decision, but there was also great consolation for some of the decisions we had made where we had been 'beating ourselves up' because we had indeed made the best decision that we could at the time.

Making important decisions can be extremely difficult. Using biblical principles to help guide those decisions is invaluable. It doesn't mean that decision-making will be easier but having sound principles to guide the process is a good thing.

An outcome of our soul-searching exercise is that King Solomon's students are now taught the principles of making wise decisions. These principles are being built into the curriculum, are displayed on the walls, and are being used in decision-making processes.

## 7 biblical principles for making wise decisions

1. What biblical principles should inform my decision?
Trust GOD from the bottom of your heart; don't try and figure out everything on your own. Listen for GOD's voice in everything you do, everywhere you go; he's the one who will keep you on track. (Proverbs 3:5-6)

2. Do I have all the facts?
Answering before listening is both stupid and rude. (Proverbs 18:13)

3. Is the pressure of time forcing me to make a decision prematurely?
Ignorant zeal is worthless; haste makes waste. (Proverbs 19:2)

4. What motives are driving my decision?
Humans are satisfied with whatever looks good; GOD probes for what is good. (Proverbs 16:2)

5. How should past experiences inform my decisions?
A quiet rebuke to a person of good sense does more than a whack on the head of a fool. (Proverbs 17:10)

6. What is the collective counsel of the wise people in my community?
Without good direction, people lose their way; the more wise
counsel you follow, the better your chances. (Proverbs 11:14)

7. Have I considered all the warning signs?
The road to life is a disciplined life; ignore correction and you're lost
for good. (Proverbs 10:17)

**Quotations from The Message**

# Dealing with Disappointments

### Q: Rueben

The school has experienced so many disappointments over the years –
prior to setting up the school, since the school opened, and now it will
be taken over by a multi-academy trust (MAT). On reflection do you
feel disappointed in God?

### A: Revd David Carr

This school started under extreme difficulties, operated for seven years
against the odds, and even now, in its seventh year, there seems to
be a change of direction outside of the original plans for the school.
Undoubtedly there have been many disappointments.

We can respond in different ways to disappointment. Our
disappointment can lead to a disengagement of our expectations,
hopes and dreams. Alternatively, we can continue to believe, despite
our disappointments, that God is in control and His purposes will
be fulfilled.

The Bible is full of people who experienced disappointment. The Israelites expected a King who would liberate them from Rome, so they were disappointed when that didn't happen. But their disappointment did not stop the purposes of God as, later, they understood that Jesus came to liberate them from sin.

God is sovereign over all things, so we must look beyond our disappointment to the creational ability of God to fulfil His purposes. Although we seldom see the future, we should not overreact to the present, but have the faith to walk into the unknown whilst depending on the sovereignty of God for the future. Remember, all things work together for good, to those who are called according to His purposes.

### A: Dr Cheron Byfield

Just to add one further observation. When we consider the followers of Jesus, they were disappointed, or shall I say, devastated when they witnessed Jesus' unjust arrest, brutal beating and horrific crucifixion on the cross. The disciples' expectations, hopes and dreams seemed to have reached a cruel dead end. But today we call those traumatic events Good Friday. Good Friday? There didn't seem to be anything good about those events when they were happening. But God was in control. His followers' disappointment and mourning were turned into joy on the third day when Jesus rose from the grave. Although disappointing at the time, Jesus' death led to the expansion of God's kingdom and the greater purposes of God being fulfilled.

## God Incidences or Coincidences

### Q: Aaron and Mayha

The book is full of extraordinary stories. On reflection, do you think they were just mere coincidences?

## A: Revd David Carr

What some would call a coincidence, many times can be traced back to a God incident . . .

Both Cheron and I have had experiences that overshadow any coincidence. Cheron being miraculously healed from cancer, Cheron bumping into the very individuals she wanted to meet at both the University of Central Florida and the University of Harvard amidst tens of thousands of people are just a few examples of extraordinary incidences in this book.

I personally have had numerous experiences where I have had to accept that this was not just a mere coincidence. I have prayed for and seen, time and time again, people healed after I've prayed for them, even from stage four cancer. Medical consultants have had to reluctantly admit that there was a God intervention after I had prayed.

When we commit our daily journey to God things are more likely to happen in our lives which are far deeper and more profound than an accidental happening. God directs the path of the righteous.

When Jesus told His disciples to find and follow a man with a water pot carried on his head, as he would have a room for them, they went looking for a man carrying a water pot on his head and, yes, he did have a room for them. Coincidence or God incident?

I often, as a hospital chaplain, find myself being directed to a different part of the hospital that I didn't plan to go to, just to find someone in desperate need of chaplaincy support. They tell me they had prayed that I would come!

One day what seemed a coincidence, will be revealed to be a fully planned God incident.

## Praise and Thanksgiving

### Q: Dinari, Joel and Crosby

Every school has its own culture. This school has a culture of praise and thanksgiving to God. Throughout the school's history it has experienced many difficult times but, despite that, the school continues to give praise and thanksgiving to God. On reflection, do you think this has had an impact on the school and, if so, how?

### A: Pastor Doreen Makaya

Praise is an expression of our faith. Praise to God should therefore never be dependent upon our circumstances, because our circumstances constantly change. So even when we find ourselves in difficult and unstable situations, we should remain steadfast in praising God because He is unchanging and His love towards us remains steadfast. So, we praise Him!

In Psalms 42 the psalmist questions why he feels so troubled, he then answers himself by saying, 'I will still praise him', in other words the praise he gave was not based on his current circumstances but on God who held the future and could not fail. The King Solomon way is to praise God because we hope in Him and not the circumstances.

This approach does not minimise or deny the seriousness of the challenge, or even that we may feel disappointed and let down. Instead, it changes our focus from ourselves and leads us to look expectantly to God. Consequently, and without even realising it, these very turbulences assisted us in developing and modelling the heart of the school Christian ethos, the Fruit of the Spirit – love, joy, peace, patience, kindness, goodness, faithfulness, gentleness and self-control. So even in the most challenging times, the school has continued to hold praise and thanksgiving services and has encouraged children to raise their voices during collective worship in song. This attitude of praise has resulted in spontaneous outbursts of praise in the corridors or canteen during lunch times and in the playground during break times. These were undisputed times of joy where many felt encouraged.

Undoubtedly giving children praise and encouragement in the classroom helps to reinforce self-esteem and positive behaviour. Similarly, the impact of praise to God at King Solomon helped to promote a positive environment. And if praise serves to empower and affirm a student's right choices, then it is reasonable to believe that praising God similarly raises faith and has the effect of affirming the choice to trust God and to rise above our circumstances.

Parents, students and visitors have often commented on the sense of wellbeing and oneness they experienced during times of celebration in the school.

Taking time out to reflect on the good things God has done for us, irrespective of what the school is going through, gives glory to God. It also aids our own wellbeing. It lifts our spirit. It moves our focus from the situation we are in and causes us to refocus on God, the one who is able to lift us out of the situation and give us hope

## A: Revd David Carr

I spent many years of my career in professional football. I noticed that when the players were having a difficult time and their supporters sang, it lifted the team's spirit and often gave them a new lease of life. By making God our focus we are able to rise above our circumstances.

It's much easier to praise someone when everything is great! But we are encouraged in our Christian faith to give thanks in all things, including when things don't go well.

## Any Regrets?

### Q: Reuben

You have been through a lot to get the school started and now you are having to hand it over to another academy trust. Do you have any regrets about starting the school?_

### A: Dr Byfield

No, no, a resounding no.

It's been an absolute honour and a privilege to have served God in establishing this unique and amazing school, and to have met so many wonderful people along the way. Students, parents, staff, politicians and government officials, Christians and non-Christians, the community.

We have achieved a great deal during the last seven years.

We have been officially rated, despite the challenges we faced, to be a 'Good' faith school. This is most unusual for a school to be rated two grades higher than its Ofsted rating, but we achieved it because we take faith seriously at King Solomon. Many expect us to be rated as an outstanding faith school at our next faith inspection.

We have been vindicated time and time again after false claims about the school or about me, and have been reported to and investigated by the authorities. No weapon formed against us prospered and all that rose up against us in judgement failed.

We were successful in obtaining approval from the Department for Education to increase the numbers of students. So, although we were initially approved to cater for just over 600 children, the successful expansion plans allow us to cater for nearly 1,300 students when we reach full capacity.

We were the first school in the country to have challenged a regulatory notice and to have got it rescinded.

We were successful in challenging government officers' practice resulting in a change in a national educational policy which now benefits all academies in the country.

We were honoured to have been chosen to be the first school in the country to install and officially unveil the new revolutionary outdoor squash court which aims to build on the excitement of the Birmingham 2022 Commonwealth Games and introduce the sport to thousands of young people. World No.5 squash player Sarah-Jane Perry and Perry the Bull – the official Commonwealth Games mascot - opened the court alongside England Squash CEO Mark Williams. The school was featured on television in the BBC news.

Although it's disappointing that we are having to transfer King Solomon to a MAT, our success is also reflected in what we are transferring.

We are transferring an Early Year's provision that is very good, a primary school that is good and a secondary school with great potential

We are transferring a school where students are generally performing well academically. Our GCSE results have improved each year.

We are transferring a school that is financially sound. At its last external audit, we had a clean set of accounts, with a very healthy cash balance. We have no material debts. No audit issues. No irregularities.

We are transferring the innovative Excell3's Student Enterprise Bank which already has over £50K, as well as school assets that can generate significant additional funds to help enterprising students get a foot up the ladder and into business ownership.

Location, location, location. We are transferring a landmark building which is strategically positioned in the Golden Mile of Birmingham. It's a huge bonus for a school positioned in the centre of Birmingham to have its own dedicated car parking facilities for 100 cars.

We are transferring a compelling vision which could enable the school to become a national centre of excellence for international business and enterprise for school-aged young people.

We are transferring through our faith authority, the Order of St Leonard, the principles of global Christian unity and oneness which is aligned to the prayer of Jesus 'that they may be one as we are one'.

We are transferring a school building that has significantly gone up in value since we purchased it seven years ago. Being in the Golden Mile there has been massive investment in the area in recent years. We bought it for about £5m, today it's worth over £20m. And we own the freehold, so we will be transferring that too. We are one of the relatively few schools in the country that owns the freehold of its school building.

We are transferring a school equipped with brand-new state-of-the-art educational facilities which can cater for nearly 1300 children. In addition, we have three fallow floors totally over 5000 square feet. There is another huge space on the fourth floor full of tens of thousands of pounds of spare furniture.

One of these floors alone would fulfil our vision to become a national centre of excellence for international business for young people. We could provide incubation facilities to enable young people to trade using a range of small office units, hot desk facilities, virtual offices, meeting rooms and accessible business storage units.

We are transferring a building which already has the space to develop a state-of-the-art Sixth Form provision offering a range of qualifications including A levels, diplomas and technical based qualifications, a Bible college, a parents college . . . the possibilities are immense.

However, by far our greatest achievement is that the school has transformed so many lives. Children, staff, parents, volunteers and consultants have grown spiritually because of this school. How can I have any regrets?

## Closing Prayers

**Students:**

Lord, we thank you for the privilege of being educated in a Christian school that encourages us to have faith in you. Of being in a school where our Christian faith is at the centre and in an environment where we are free to talk about God.

We thank you for nurturing our character so that we demonstrate the Fruit of the Spirit. We pray that our character will continue to develop so that we become more like Jesus.

Thank you for our parents who chose to send us to King Solomon. Thank you for our fellow students and the friendships we have formed.

Thanks for our teachers and school chaplains for our celebration and collective worship services. They are a special part of our school life.

And, Lord, we thank you for loving us. We know we can put our trust and faith in you as you love us more than anyone else.

**Revd David Carr:**

Almighty God, we thank you for all that has been achieved over the last seven years and for your Holy Spirit who directs our paths and fulfils your purposes for our future.

We pray that King Solomon International Business School's spiritual and academic future will be secure in your purposes.

We pray for Dr Cheron who you used to birth the vision for this school against many challenges. Over the years she has been misrepresented and misjudged, but I pray that she may see the vision continue to transform the lives of students in the school.

**Dr Cheron Byfield:**

Lord, I thank you for all those who have been called to serve in and around the school to fulfil your purposes. May they be spiritually strong, increase in wisdom and be salt and light to those around them as they continue to serve you.

Lord, I pray for all the students at King Solomon, our alumni and those who will join the school in the future. I humbly ask that you bless them all and that the vision of the school will be fulfilled in them, so that they achieve educational excellence, develop their character, are equipped to live, work and trade in the global economy and are successful.

I pray that the students will be strong and courageous, never afraid or discouraged from doing good and that you will be their spiritual satnav, directing them and fulfilling your purposes wherever they go.

And I pray, that when you look at King Solomon, even with all its imperfections, you will say, 'This is my beloved school in whom I am well pleased.'

**Pastor Doreen Makaya:**

Dear Father,

Thank you for your faithfulness and love towards King Solomon School, for always making a way in times of challenge. We pray for the staff that you will continue to bless them with strength and courage. Remind them that they need not fear or be dismayed, because you are with them. We pray for steadfastness, boldness and bravery in the face of change. Help them to pursue what is right even if unpopular, and to be strong on hard days and peacemakers in all things.

Thank you for our parents and carers, for their perseverance and faith. We pray for their continued support of pupils and in the building of strong working relations with teachers and staff. Lord, surround them with your love, joy, and peace.

**And they all said:**

We pray this in the precious name of Jesus.

Amen!

# Endpiece

Through the doors and out of the gates. Not quite for the last time. But nearly.

The end was not in question though.

The focus of the last few months had been on transferring King Solomon to a multi-academy trust. But the Christian faith designation of the school and the vision had been secured. There was much to thank God for.

No doubt King Solomon will continue to face battles, as Christianity will always be under attack. There has been and most probably will continue to be occasional defeats on the way to victory, but defeats would be just that . . . occasional. God has and will always have the final say. And Jesus has already won the war.

So many heroes have worked tirelessly with Cheron since the school opened seven years ago. Seven years? How they have flown by. Seven years! There is spiritual significance to the number seven in scripture. That's the biblical number for completion. Has this phase of the school's development been completed in its seventh year? Is it a coincidence that this book of King Solomon's story is being launched in the school's seventh year?

So much has been achieved in the last seven years, and the reality is no one knows all the lives that have been impacted and transformed. There remains a strong belief that from this school will emerge young people that will do great things for the Kingdom of God, that good seeds have been planted in students' lives that will show themselves in years to come. All those who have stood in prayer and contributed to the school have played a significant part in the successes of this school.

The school will go forward. It will continue to be salt and light. The Christian ethos will impact more lives. The vision will endure. The children will excel.

Cheron started up the engine, moved into first gear and drove forward. Driving forward. Something she had been doing all her life.

She wasn't about to stop.

# The Students Who Started The Journey:

Thank you to the founding students who made King Solomon International Business School possible.

## The Founding primary phase students of 2015:

Mercy, AaRon, ShaRon, Badiu, Bell, Ayaana, Binns, Lela, Nevaeha, Joshua, Zemari, Ariana, Keeandre, Chaundae, Kacie, Junior, Keiondre, Z'Kye, Aya, Kiara, Akaiyo, Nylah, Amoii, Amelie, Mace, Manning, Mehkile, Charlotte, Josiha, Nylah, William, Sofija, Nathan, Zariah, Jasmine, Elizabeth, Joshua, Shay, Amelia, Issac, Rico, Shiloh, Elim, Niamh, Kaeden, Abbas, Olivia, Roberts Kocean, Emnet, Michaela, Kabonesa, Italy, Milan, MyRon, Kimora, Lannaya, Elim.

## The Founding secondary phase students of 2015:

Derek, Emmanuel, Anuoluwapo, Lucian, Charnai, Muhammed, Romalia, Adonis, Sophia, Zaynah, Victor, DeRon, Kymar, Billie, Hadija, Kaydon, Kyle, Ayanna, Corriann, Leiyah, Jamar, Khyrell, Rebecca, Tionne, Aneika, Arian, Jumanni, Matthew, Desharn, Deshaun, Lauren, Celia, Miracle, Josiah, Samuel, Aurora, Moria, Leah, Tyhesia, Dibora, Preacious, Shonese, Bryanna, Malachi, Nia, Tyanna, Rhianna, Alexander, Farrell, Reuben, Tiarni, Nniah-Asia, Shannay, Stephen, Kimarni, Robel, Charisma, Ashan, Kanye, Malachi, Lwazi, Isaiah, Rebecca, Jahmel, Jamel, Kaylah, Alexander, Sean, Damarae, Mariyah, Johnathan, Zoriah, Leah, J'leol, Tierre, Ryan, Danyal, Abejai, Favour, Thierry, Kejai, Ra'marn, Nathanael, Michaela, Ricardo, Kwaku, Malayha, Darnell, Aariyah, Lily, Onan, Safa, Sana.

# Other Books By Ralph

Ralph is a Christian author who specialises in biographies and ghost-written autobiographies. His books include:

*Working for God*

*God-Life*

*Cheating Death, Living Life – Linda's Story* (with Linda Huskisson)

*Gerald Coates – Pioneer*

*The Power Partnership* (with Jonathan Conrathe)

*Faith Man – Wild Adventures with a Faithful God* (with David Lamb)

*Greater Things – The Story of New Wine* (with Paul Harcourt)

*Embrace the Journey – Becky Murray's Story* (with Becky Murray)

*Returning the Lost Smiles – One Man's Fight Against Leprosy* (with Amar Timalsina)